YOU KNOW?

FASCINATING FACTS & FALLACIES ABOUT BUSINESS

D. Keith Denton / Charles Boyd

PRENTICE HALL
Englewood Cliffs, New Jersey 07632

Prentice-Hall International (UK) Limited, *London*
Prentice-Hall of Australia Pty. Limited, *Sydney*
Prentice-Hall Canada, Inc., *Toronto*
Prentice-Hall Hispanoamericana, S.A., *Mexico*
Prentice-Hall of India Private Limited, *New Delhi*
Prentice-Hall of Japan, Inc., *Tokyo*
Simon & Schuster Asia Pte. Ltd., *Singapore*
Editora Prentice-Hall do Brasil, Ltda., *Rio de Janeiro*

© 1994 by
PRENTICE-HALL

10 9 8 7 6 5 4 3 2 1

Library of Congress Cataloging-in-Publication Data

Denton, D. Keith.
    Did you know? : fascinating facts and fallacies about business /
D. Keith Denton, Charles Boyd.
        p.   cm.
    Includes bibliographical references.
    ISBN 0–13–032194–X
    1. Business—Miscellanea.   I. Boyd, Charles.   II. Title.
HF5341.D46   1994
650—dc20   93–47947
                                                                CIP

ISBN 0-13-032194-X

PRENTICE HALL
Career and Personal Development
Englewood Cliffs, NJ 07632

Simon & Schuster, A Paramount Communications Company

Printed in the United States of America

Introduction

Despite what you might think, all the following statements are *false*. If you doubt it, look inside the book:

■ Foreign assignments help your career. (p. 6–7)

■ Buying an American car keeps jobs in the United States. (p. 140)

■ U.S. workers receive more pay than their counterparts in Japan and Germany. (p. 62)

■ *Fortune* 500 companies create most of the jobs in the United States. (p. 186–87)

■ The most powerful and dynamic country in the world is not Japan nor is it the United States. (p. 107)

On the other hand, what is true may shock or surprise you. For example,

■ Ninety-nine percent good service means 20,000 wrong drug prescriptions each year. (p. 183)

■ Only 55% of Americans are prepared for their jobs. (p. 204)

■ Small businesses create most of the jobs. (p. 170)

■ There are 700 plastic flamingos for every live one in the United States. (p. 16)

■ Your best customers are those who complain. (p. 26)

This book is about careers and consumers. It is about customer service and ethics. It is about compensation, competition, and jobs. It is about large and small businesses. It is about technology and society. In short, it is about business and you. Take a look inside. You will find some surprising facts and fallacies.

For instance, if the earth's population were reduced to only 1,000 people while their ethnic mix remained the same, how many of them would be like you? Do you know how many times a day organizations access information about you and your family from some computer database? How does the United States really compare with other nations in today's global economic competition? What are the facts behind the health care cost monster we are trying to tame? Is the condition of our economy as bad as you hear?

Each day we read and hear information about these and other key business and economic issues, but much of it is outdated or simply fallacies rather than facts. Business fallacies affect each of us in our roles as customers, employees, bosses, or teachers. What we believe to be true about business and economics influences the way we earn and spend our money, pay our taxes, and vote. Business touches key areas of our lives in profound ways. For this reason, we tried to unearth information that may change the way you think about business. One thing is sure: Business is anything but dull.

You can explore the book in any order you choose. Those who want to know where we got these facts will find that a reference number in parentheses follows each fact. A page number also appears when appropriate. Simply find the matching number in the References section in the back of the book to find the source of the fact.

Facts need not be dry or overly serious to be valuable. We hope that you will find the ones in this book interesting, intriguing, stunning, funny, and in some cases irreverent.

We believe the book will be of value to business students, practitioners, customers, workers, teachers, and anyone wanting to learn about business. It will be useful to the public speaker looking for facts with which to drive home key points. Everyone reading this book will, we hope, relate to at least one of these groups. We certainly mean to exclude no one.

Acknowledgments

We thank Ellen Schneid Coleman of Prentice Hall for her encouragement and guidance throughout this project. Barbara Palumbo and her staff at Prentice Hall created the final graphic work and typesetting of the text. Their efforts and those of the copyeditor, Sally Ann Bailey, greatly improved the book. Our special thanks go to Lynn Grable. Lynn turned our scribblings into legible copy and provided initial graphics for the text. She kept track of the many word processing files a book of this type requires and reorganized them for us countless times. Without her skill and patience with us, this book would have been much harder to write. And that's a fact.

Contents

Accounting

Fallacy: Return on investment (ROI) is the ultimate measure of corporate success.

Fact: According to Carl Thor, president of the American Productivity and Quality Center, ROI is misleading and often useless. He notes that financial analysts try to remove, or at least explain, special write-offs and windfalls, inventory adjustments, foreign currency translation, and the effects of acquisitions and divestitures, but that the search for true earning eludes many insiders. Furthermore, trying to compare earnings between American and Japanese corporations is basically guesswork.

Thor also notes that the "I" in ROI is even more suspect. Companies can show a loss even in good years if a firm changes the way it values its assets and charges depreciation against them. He said, "Investment on an unadjusted balance sheet is misleading *except* for the newest of companies where inflation has not yet had time to erode the purchasing power of their *vintage dollars*." His solution is to "stop using ROI as the best single indicator of performance." Also, he suggests using other measures of growth, quality, productivity, market share, new contracts/products, and so on. (389)

——————

93% According to a survey of U.S. manufacturers, over 93% of them still use direct labor as an overhead allocation base even though direct labor has been shown to be either inaccurate or a *minor* portion of product cost for many companies. (346, p. 19)

Let's get rid of "overhead." Carl Thor notes an "incredible assumption" about overhead in accounting systems. We assume overhead is best related to direct labor cost. Thus overhead becomes a "burden" to direct labor hours. For example, if direct labor is $10.00 an hour, then we automatically add an additional amount, let's say $35.00, to cover overhead. Now direct labor suddenly costs $45.00 and distorts decision making. He says if the pieces of this overhead were analyzed, they would more likely be related to things other than direct labor, such as machine use, total people employed, hours of operation, number of products or parts run, number of announced corporate visits, and so on. He notes activity-based cost *(ABC) accounting* helps sort out these overhead pieces. (391)

Some U.S. manufacturers still firmly believe that an abundance of inventory adds to the firm's value and is one of the main indicators for determining how well a business is doing. (ABC accounting challenges these assumptions.) (347, p. 73)

Acquisitions and Mergers

Fallacy: It's primarily employees and entry-level people who lose their jobs in mergers and acquisitions.

Fact: True, organizations will sometimes terminate thousands of employees after a merger or acquisition, but studies also indicate that 58% of managers in an acquired firm are gone within five years and 47% of senior managers are gone within one year. (311)

2% **Fallacy:** Most acquisitions in the United States during the 1980s came from corporate raiders.

Fact: A review of 150 hostile bids since 1983 showed that they represented *only 2%* of acquisitions made or attempted, and only half of them came from raiders. (44, p. 89)

Fallacy: The growing number of strategic alliances among firms must mean that they achieve what the management in those companies involved wanted from them.

Fact: The number of joint ventures between U.S.- and foreign-owned companies grew 27% a year from 1985 through 1992. However, about one-third of 49 alliances studied by the McKinsey management consulting firm did not meet top management's expectations. (177, p. 77)

Banking

1 in 4 One-fourth of our business loans come from foreign sources. (427)

Fallacy: The Japanese continue to buy a larger percentage of U.S. Treasury securities.

Fact: From 1989 through early 1992, net purchases of these securities by the Japanese fell 34%. Purchases by U.S. banks rose 35% during this period. (121)

Fallacy: Banks *are* conservative investors, especially after S&L failures.

Fact: One estimate says banks are making $600 billion in risky loans to developing countries for commercial real estate ventures and loans for leveraged buyouts. Banks are writing off $20 billion of these loans each year, which is five times as much as in the early 1980s. More than 1,000 of our 12,000 commercial banks are in trouble. (401)

Fallacy: Since the savings and loan association failures, banks are more secure, less likely to fail.

Fact: Between 1943 and 1975 there were fewer than 10 bank failures per year. Between 1975 and 1981 there were fewer than 20 per year. There were 206 failures in 1989, 168 in 1990, and 127 in 1991. (401)

Fallacy: We need not worry about bank failures because the Federal Deposit Insurance Corporation (FDIC) insures each deposit up to $100,000.

Fact: As of October 1992, the FDIC had about $5 billion, but all of it was committed to banks it knew were going to fail. (446)

———

Fallacy: Almost every American family has a checking account.

Fact: The banks wish that were true! But only three out of four families do. (121)

———

 It is no fallacy: Education pays. Banks are hiring about 20% of their new employees at the high school level; 10 years ago, the proportions would have been reversed with as many as 80% of newly hired workers having no more than a high school education. (240, p. 241)

———

 Sanwa Bank in Japan recently sought new business by encouraging patrons to open savings accounts in the names of their pets. These new accounts come complete with a passbook and a book that contains customer information and a photo of the pet. The pet's owner must pay the taxes on the interest the account earns. Beats burying bones in the backyard as a savings plan! (463, pp. 17–18)

Career and Promotions

Fallacy: Successful managers give a lot of time and attention to the traditional management activities of planning, decision making, controlling, motivating, staffing, and training.

Fact: Even though formal personnel policies say it, new management trainees are told it, and every management textbook says it is what *should* happen, a study of both successful and effective managers found that *successful* managers spent relatively more time and effort socializing, politicking, and interacting with outsiders than did their less successful counterparts. Just as important, successful managers did not give much time or attention to the traditional management activities of planning, decision making, and controlling or to the human resource management activities of motivating/reinforcing, staffing, training/developing, and managing conflict. On the other hand, *effective* (as opposed to successful) managers' activities consisted of communication and human resource management. These areas of focus made by far the largest relative contribution to a manager's effectiveness, whereas management concepts, including networking, made by far the least contribution. (Note: In the study, successful managers were isolated by dividing a manager's level in the organization by his or her length of service. The study defined effectiveness as (1) getting the job done through high quantity and quality standards and (2) getting the job done through people.) (317)

Fallacy: Overseas and foreign assignments are a good career move.

6

Fact: A good manager in the United States does not always make a good manager abroad. A study of 80 U.S. multinational companies found failure rates of 10–20%, with 7% of the firms having recall rates of 30%. Failure was defined as the inability of an expatriate to perform effectively in a foreign country and hence the need for the employee to be fired or recalled home. Thus, in some firms, almost one-third of foreign assignments resulted in a career self-destruct. (310, p. 117)

 General Motors (GM) may not always understand what its American customer wants, but it does recognize the importance of foreign culture and customers. Although GM was cutting costs in the early 1990s, it still spent almost $500,000 annually to teach 150 Americans relocating overseas about the culture to which they would be moving. This training has helped prevent frustrated employees from returning to the United States earlier than planned. GM's premature return rate is only 1%, which is much better than the 25% rate at companies that take less care in selecting and training employees going overseas. (135)

CEOs

Fallacy: Hire an "outsider" for your chief executive officer if you want your business to do well.

Fact: A. T. Kearney's research on successful and run-of-the-mill *Fortune* 500 companies discovered that CEOs of top-performing companies had one unique characteristic. *All but one* had been appointed from *inside* the company and had been the CEO for more than 16 years. (332, p. 58)

Fallacy: CEOs tend to be promoted from inside the organization.

Fact: Each year about 10–15% of major U.S. corporations exchange their CEOs. Of that group, the vast majority (80–85%) select their new CEO from *outside* their organization. (314)

 In 1990 the average chief executive of a major U.S. corporation received 85 times the pay of the typical American worker. In Japan, the average boss receives only 17 times the pay of an ordinary worker. (262, p. 93)

Fallacy: CEOs have always made a lot more than lower-echelon personnel.

Fact: The gap was not nearly as wide as it is today. At the start of 1980, the boss's average paycheck was 42 times the pay of the

8

ordinary worker; 10 years later it had risen to the current 85 times. (Some sources believe it is closer to 119 times.) (262, p. 95)

⸻

Fallacy: American CEOs' pay raises are comparable to the raises factory workers receive.

Fact: In 1960, the average U.S. CEO of an American nonfinancial corporation earned 12 times what a factory worker earned, after taxes. By 1990, that multiple was 93 times. (1, p. 7)

⸻

Fallacy: The high pay of American CEOs is a problem only in large companies.

Fact: The average CEO of a midsized company in the United States makes 54% more than his or her counterpart in Canada. (18)

⸻

■ The typical U.S. CEO of a company with annual sales of $250 million earns $543,000 total compensation. A similar Japanese CEO earns $352,000, or about half what his or her American counterpart earns. The American CEO earns 90% more than a British or German CEO and 400% more than a Korean executive. And the American can buy three times as much with a dollar as can the Japanese executive and twice what a German executive can. (20, p. 205)

⸻

The peeled perk: One executive of a large advertising agency used to have a butler deliver him a peeled orange each day. A newspaper reported the cost of this delivery to be about $300 per day, or $80,000 a year. (144, p. 194)

⸻

A survey of 1,535 senior chief financial officers reports that their average 1991 salary and bonus was $129,700—just half the average for chief executive officers. (105)

Fallacy: CEOs usually do not have their performance evaluated and don't want it evaluated!

Fact: It's true for Japanese executives, but not for American executives. One survey by the *Los Angeles Times* shows that 59% of U.S. chief executives have their performance measured at least once a year. On the other hand, only 2% of Japan's top managers are measured in this way. An additional 45% of American executives support this evaluation process, while none of the Japanese executives supports it. (411)

———

Fallacy: Effective CEOs manage by carefully organizing their workdays, being sure to reserve large chunks of private time for strategic thinking and other top management duties.

Fact: This fallacy persists though good studies of how CEOs use their time dating back to 1973 tell us otherwise. Effective CEOs manage by the *interruption.* They remain open to the phone calls and visits that constantly interrupt their work. This keeps them in touch with what is going on in their organizations and helps them build a web of important relationships. They find the larger chunks of time they need for reflective thinking early in the morning or at night. (67)

Communication

Fallacy: Top managers keep close contact with their workers.

Fact: According to employee benefits consulting firm Foster Higgins and Company, only 45% of large employers make regular use of worker opinion surveys (probably the most obvious means of communicating employee concerns). (233, p. 57)

In 1988, the Opinion Research Corporation of Chicago surveyed 100,000 middle managers and technical, clerical, and hourly workers of *Fortune* 500 companies. Except in the sales group, employees believed top management was less willing to listen to their problems than they were five years earlier. (233, p. 57)

Fallacy: Top managers communicate with their employees.

Fact: Ninety-seven percent of the CEOs surveyed by management consulting firm Foster Higgins said communicating with employees has a positive impact on job satisfaction, and 79% think it benefits the bottom line. But *only 22%* actually do it weekly or more often. (233, p. 70)

Fewer than half the employees polled in a 1990 study by consultants Towers Perrin believe managers are aware of their employee problems. (230)

11

In a research study by the Hay Group, *only 34%* of 1 million employees in over 2,000 organizations responded favorably to questions about how well their company listens to them. (230)

 Toll-free 800 telephone numbers first became available in the United States in 1967. The number of calls per year to 800 numbers rose from 7 million that first year to 11 billion in 1992. (147)

 Fallacy: There are about the same number of languages in the world as there are nations.

Fact: There are over 8,000 natural languages, but only 200 nations. (15, p. 269)

Fallacy: In this information age, managers have no shortage of information about their business.

Fact: A 1990 survey by Dunhill Personnel System Incorporated and the Columbia University Business School found "lack of information" to be the number one source of on-the-job stress for middle managers. (191, p. 131)

∎ A communication network that combined fiber optics and coaxial cable could transmit the equivalent of 30,000 single-spaced, typewritten pages. That is 500 times more than a telephone line carries. (459, p. 112)

Consumer Life-styles (American)

Fallacy: The labor-saving devices and technology we have at home today reduce the amount of work one does at home.

Fact: Among the many appliances in the home, only the microwave oven has reduced labor time during recent years. Before then, weekly food preparation time declined by almost 10 hours between the 1920s and the 1960s. But more time spent for shopping, doing home management tasks, and child care offset the gains. Some labor-saving devices saved time in one task while increasing it in others. For example, the refrigerator saved time by eliminating the need for daily shopping and for storing ice at home, but it resulted in the loss of door-to-door vendors and created a need for the supermarket. That meant more travel time to self-service food stores. (47, p. 88) Other modern appliances increased working time by raising standards of cleanliness. (47, p. 89)

Fallacy: The 1950s were the "good ol' days."

Fact: Not if you are talking about physical labor around the home. In 1953 only 24% of American homes had kitchen ranges; today, over 97% have them. In those "good ol' days," only 1.3% of American homes were air conditioned; today, 64% of our homes are air conditioned. In 1953 only 3% of American homes had dishwashers; today, 43% are so equipped. (47, p. 111)

13

▪ Each day members of the Prodigy online service, a joint venture of IBM and Sears, write about 65,000 electronic mail messages and post an average of 80,000 messages to the service's many bulletin boards. (175, p. 100)

Fallacy: Child neglect and less time spent with children are products of our rushed pace and the long workweeks required in modern society.

Fact: There was much less emotional attachment to children before the sixteenth century in Europe than there is today. The rich had little to do with their children until they were grown. Nurses cared for them as infants, and their parents later sent them away to school. In all income groups, parents often left their children unattended for long periods of time. Swaddling, which meant wrapping babies in cloths that *immobilized* their limbs, was common practice during the first months of a child's life. Another practice was to rock a baby hard, after which they would remain still and quiet, causing no distraction to adults as they worked. Poor working women who needed to sustain their families could not afford to pay anyone to take care of their children. It was not uncommon for these mothers to give their children a dose of opium to keep them in a stupor while they were left completely unattended. Child neglect during these times was a contributor to infant mortality. These conditions changed little until the nineteenth century. (47, pp. 92–93)

 A sign of Americans' insecurity? The number of security guards in the United States doubled between 1970 and 1990, rising to 2.6% of the work force. Among government workers, the number of prison guards doubled from 1960 to 1980, and then doubled again between 1980 and 1990. What does this say about our society? (1, p. 269)

 With the health concerns about smoking, you might suspect that it would be hard to sell cigarettes with the brand name Death. But smokers bought 700,000 packs under that brand name during the first year after it was introduced. (121) And just when you thought you were beginning to understand Americans!

———

Fallacy: Today we have more leisure time than ever before.

Fact: One survey revealed that after work and household duties, Americans have fewer than 17 hours per week of "leisure," and it's worse for women, who still do most of the housework. (359, p. 13)

———

Fallacy: Europeans, with a more leisure-oriented life-style than Americans, naturally spend more time shopping and browsing.

Fact: Americans spend three to four times as many shopping hours a year as West Europeans do. Also, consider that

∎ There are about 16 square feet of shopping center space for every American. (47, p. 107)

∎ Americans in every income class own about twice as much in material goods as they did 40 years ago. (47, p. 109)

———

Fallacy: Overwork is the main factor that creates job stress for managers.

Fact: Not according to a 1990 survey of 255 middle managers conducted by Dunhill Personnel System and the Columbia University Business School. They found that overwork ranked third. Lack of information was the most stressful factor, followed by corporate indecision. (191, p. 131)

———

California livin': One out of 10 Californians owns a convertible; 1 out of 3 has earthquake insurance. (90)

∎ You can believe those jokes about giving dad a tie for Father's Day. In the United States, dads get 12,600 miles of ties on their special day each year. Neckties predominate; only 180 miles of the total are bow ties. (121)

———

There are 700 plastic flamingos for every live 1 in the United States. (89) (It is hard to get a live flamingo to stand still in your yard.)

———

 See what you can do when you learn to write? Baseball pitcher Nolan Ryan autographed an estimated 90,000 baseballs, photos, and posters during the 1991–1992 winter. For this he earned an estimated $1,800,000! (42)

———

Fallacy: Americans who pay a lot for an automobile buy luxury sedans or expensive sports cars.

Fact: Those types of vehicles may have become too expensive for many car buyers during the recession of the early 1990s. In mid-1992, the best-selling consumer product in the United States priced above $20,000 was the Ford Explorer. (179, p. 16)

———

 Hank Williams, Jr., sings a song in which he encourages listeners to "come on over to the country." Perhaps many are doing so; at least, they are moving away from rock music. In 1986, rock music accounted for 47% of record sales. By mid-1992, rock music was down to 36% of sales. (42)

———

 From 1987 to 1991, the cost of feeding an airline passenger rose 42%, from $4.03 to $5.73. (60) That's a lot of peanuts.

It's such a hassle to take out the trash! Laws allow New York City to sell its garbage to other municipalities. Some days it's just plain harder to do than it is on other days.

On Friday, July 10, 1992, a train hauling carloads of New York City trash arrived in Kansas City, Kansas. The trash was loaded onto 99 trucks and driven to the Clinton, Missouri, landfill about 100 miles away, where it had been accepted. But after only 7 of the trucks were unloaded, a rainstorm created muddy roads that brought the project to a halt. The truck drivers transported the rest of the refuse back to Kansas City where it was loaded back onto the train. With most of its unwanted, smelly, bug-infested load restored, the train pulled out of Kansas City for parts unknown. (69)

———

 Until early 1992, state welfare recipients enrolled in a job-training program run by the state of Oregon's Adult and Family Services Division had an extra benefit. The agency paid their traffic tickets! During the last year this benefit existed, the agency made full or partial payments on about 117 citations, including two for drunken driving. Public opinion convinced the agency to stop paying these citations. (124, p. 112)

———

Fallacy: Americans see a bleak outlook for their futures.

Fact: They are pessimistic about the *economy's* future, but not about their future. A nationwide poll conducted for *Fortune* magazine in 1992 showed that 55% of those surveyed were pessimistic about the U.S. economy's future, but *89%* were *optimistic* about their own careers and financial prospects. (132, p. 48)

———

Fallacy: The welfare system is the chief cause of the rise in single-parent families in the United States.

Fact: The facts indicate that the welfare system's impact has been minor. Three economic changes during the 1970s and 1980s are more important reasons for the rise in single-parent families: (1) the earnings of less educated men fell sharply, making them poorer breadwinners; (2) competition from lower-cost labor abroad drove down wages in the United States; and (3) women's wages rose to an all-time high of 71% of men's wages by 1990, making women less dependent on men as wage earners. (140, p. 91)

Fallacy: Rock music is the most popular type of music in the United States.

Fact: Two out of three Americans *do not* consider themselves to be rock fans. (148) There is no predominantly popular music form in the United States today. (149, pp. A1, A8)

∎ Want to be a millionaire? Try smoking an expensive cigar. One of every three cigars costing more than $1.25 will be smoked by a millionaire. (148)

Fallacy: Wealthy Americans who became richer during the 1980s increased their contributions to charity.

Fact: Total giving from all sources more than doubled during the 1980s, but the portion given by the rich fell. The number of Americans earning $1 million or more rose 14-fold during the decade, but their collective giving rose only 500%. This resulted in a *60% average per person drop in giving* among members of this group. (154, p. 92) Wonder if they have ever heard Glen Fry's song "I got mine."

Fallacy: More U.S. citizens own their own homes than do the citizens of any other country.

Fact: Taiwan leads with 79.1% of homes owned by occupants. *The United States ranks ninth* with its 63.5% share of homes owned by occupants. (157)

Fallacy: Rising sales of electronic car alarm systems are a major deterrent to auto thefts.

Fact: The number of stolen cars continues to climb, and the proportion of cars stolen rose from 1 in 151 in 1981 to 1 in 119 in 1992. Half of stolen cars are *unlocked.* Thieves find a key in the ignition switch of 1 of 5 cars they steal. (171)

———

One in 10 Americans receives food stamps. (173)

———

 As baby boomers hit their midforties, they seem to be turning from tennis to the less physically demanding game of golf. The number of golfers in the United States rose 22% from 1987 through 1991 and rose another 7.7% in 1992 as the recession slowed golf equipment sales. (178)

———

 Bumper crop: If the candy corn produced in the United States each year were made into ears of corn, it would make 2,250,000 ears. (Sorry about the corny joke.) (188)

———

∎ Here's a story of true grit. "Hominy" people do you think attended the World Grits Festival in St. George, South Carolina, in the spring of 1992? The answer: 60,000. (161)

———

Fallacy: Most African Americans and whites watch the same TV shows in the United States.

Fact: None of the 10 TV shows most often watched by African Americans are also most often watched by whites. (161)

Consumer Life-styles
(Foreign)

The average U.S. supermarket stocked about 9,000 different products in 1976. By 1992, most carried over 30,000 items. (450, p. 24)

Fallacy: Japanese success means that Japanese people believe they are enjoying the "good life."

Fact: Many of them disagree. Japanese responding to a survey for the 1992 *World Competitiveness Report* rated their quality of life below that enjoyed in every European country except Portugal. These results are more dramatic when you consider that the respondents worked for the larger Japanese firms in which jobs are most secure. (165, p. 59)

———

A square meter of commercial property in downtown Tokyo costs as much as $300,000. (340, p. 48) The average price of a small condominium in Tokyo rose to $471,000 (roughly 10 times the average working man's salary). (340)

———

The average price of a small condominium in Tokyo rose to $471,000 (roughly 10 times the average working man's salary). (340)

Keep circling the block! You can be fined up to $1,400 for parking overnight illegally in Tokyo. (85)

Japan is the undisputed vending machine capital of the world. There is 1 vending machine for every 23 people (U.S. ratio is 1 for every 42). What can you buy from a vending machine in Japan? How about a pearl necklace, freeze-dried noodles with hot water, and chopsticks! Some 195,000 machines even sell alcohol. (239)

Cheaper chip shots for the Japanese? Japan's tumbling Nikkei stock market in 1992 gave avid Japanese golfers one benefit. The price for 10-year memberships in some Japanese golf clubs fell from $391,000 to a mere $200,000. These memberships are actually investments that owners trade much like stocks and bonds. To actually play on a club's course, you must register at the club by anteing up an additional one-time fee of about $30,000. Tennis anyone? (126)

Japan's birth rate per 1,000 is 10.2 compared to 16.2 in the United States. Why? In 1989, 37% of 25- to 29-year-old Japanese women are single. That compares to 21% in 1975. Many men work to 9 or 10 P.M. and commute to and from work for another hour to an hour and a half. (282)

Fallacy: Hard work never hurt anyone.

Fact: It does in Japan, where *karoshi*—sudden death from a heart attack or stroke caused by overwork—is common. Each year, 10,000 Japanese die from karoshi. (158)

Filling a hole in the heart: that is the sales strategy of Saluski Oiwa, president of Japan Efficiency Headquarters (JEH), a Tokyo employment company. The firm rents actors to pose as the son or daughter of Japanese parents whose real sons or daughters are too busy with their careers to pay mom and dad a visit. JEH charges $385 for a five-hour visit from a "son" or "daughter," and $769 for a couple, and will add a rental baby or child for a total of $1,155. How do parents respond to a visit from these actors? One retired carpenter enjoyed it so much he thought he might pay for another visit rather than spend for a vacation for himself and his wife.

JEH also has customers who are grown children who pay for visits from surrogate parents. (125)

Talk about car pooling. In the United States, there is 1 car for every 1.7 people. In China, there is 1 for every 679 people. (138)

∎ Is consumerism becoming the universal language? Since 1970, China has increased beer production per capita 372%. Since 1979, wine consumption in France has dropped 42%, while frozen food consumption has risen 463%. (148)

With all its diversity and problems, maybe the Russian Bear should be exchanged for an octopus. Anyone who thinks that *Russia* is (or was) one monolithic nation needs to consider these facts:

∎ In the U.S.S.R's 1989 census, ethnic Russians were barely half the population.

∎ Less than half the non-Russian population has a command of the Russian language.

■ The Russian population rose by 27% between 1959 and 1989, but the Muslim population grew by *125%*. The ratio of Russians to Muslims is 2.6 to 1. Russia today has more than 55 million Muslims, more than Egypt, Turkey, and Iran combined. (5, pp. 121–122)

Not only is life hard in Russia these days, it is also short. Soviet death rates for people in their forties rose by over one-fifth between 1969 and 1970 and 1984 and 1985. For people in their fifties, it rose by over one-fourth during those years. Soviet life expectancy at birth fell by almost three years for both men and women between the mid-1960s and the mid-1980s. (5, p. 124)

Hungary for love? An average of 17,800 Harlequin Romance novels were sold per day in Hungary during 1991. (86)

Fifty percent of *all* Mexicans have a close relative living in the United States. (408)

■ Waiting for a very high tide? There are two subscribers to *Surfer* magazine who live in Saudi Arabia. (148)

Now that's progress! In New Zealand, there are 70 million sheep, *only* 3 million people, but already 32 Pizza Huts. (238)

It is said that everyone has his or her price, and apparently it is pretty low in China. The Chinese government pays certain scholars and scientists a $20 monthly bonus to discourage them from moving to another country. (148)

Corporations

Fallacy: When it comes to corporations, the rich get richer and the big get bigger.

Fact: Between 1984 and 1989, 143 corporations disappeared from the *Fortune* 500, and many others downsized. (329)

———

Fallacy: *Fortune* 500 companies create most U.S. jobs.

Fact: *Fortune* 500 companies eliminated 3.4 million jobs between 1980 and 1990. During that period, companies with fewer than 500 employees created over 13 million jobs. (104, p. 50)

———

 In 1970, 64 of the world's largest 100 industrial corporations were based in the United States, 26 were in Europe, and 8 were in Japan. By 1988, 42 were in the United States, 33 in Europe, and 15 in Japan. (100, p. 30)

Customer Complaints

Fallacy: Once a customer becomes upset or unhappy with a service, you might as well go on to the next customer because you have lost that one.

Fact: When employees handle complaints properly, it can significantly affect a business's earnings. A national consumer survey reported a strong positive relationship between complaining and brand loyalty. Where employees resolved minor losses ($1–5) to the customer's satisfaction, 70% of the complainers reported they would maintain brand loyalty. Where there were major complaints (financial loss of over $100), 54% of complainers stayed brand loyal *if employees handled their complaints well.* Even where one of these high-loss complainers' problems was not resolved, 19% expressed a desire to repurchase. But here is the real surprise from the survey: Only *9% of noncomplainers* would continue to purchase offending products and services. The conclusion is that not only should you try to satisfy customer complaints, you should make it easy to complain. Solicit complaints, since noncomplainers just quit buying your product or service without complaining. (209, p. 6)

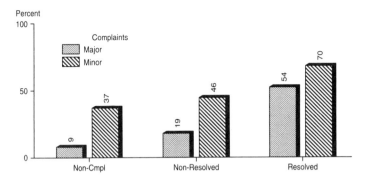

U.S. Office of Consumer Affairs, "Increasing Consumer Complaints"

Fallacy: Making it easy for customers to complain about the goods or services they receive is only asking for trouble.

Fact: A federal study found that encouraging customer complaints increased the likelihood of those customers doing business with an organization. If the company responded immediately, apologized, and guaranteed to fix it, the possibility of the customer remaining a customer rose to *95%*. (28)

Fallacy: Complaint-handling centers are an *overhead* cost for doing business.

Fact: Complaint-handling units are *profit* centers. The U.S. Office of Consumer Affairs reported the high return on investment from corporate complaint-handling units ranged from 15% for package goods to 400% for retailing. (209, p. 9)

 A variety of marketplace surveys found the following facts:

▪ Dissatisfied customers tell an average of *10* other people about their negative experience.

▪ Satisfied customers tell an average of 5 other people about their positive experience. (201)

Fallacy: It is the "old people," the grumps, who complain.

Fact: The young are more likely to complain than are the elderly. (211, p. 2)

━━━━━

70% The U.S. Office of Consumer Affairs reported that their National Consumer Survey found that nearly one-third of the households interviewed had experienced at least one significant consumer problem during the year preceding the survey. The startling aspect of the survey was the finding that 70% of the respondents with service problems did not complain because they did not feel it would be worth their time, they believed complaining would not do any good, or they did not know how or when to complain. (209, p. 3)

━━━━━

26 to 1 The White House Office of Consumer Affairs estimates that for every complaint a company receives, there are 26 other unsatisfied customers who do not complain. (28)

━━━━━

▪ Fewer than 5% of the complaints about large-ticket, durable goods or services ever reach the manufacturer. (210)

━━━━━

 About 41% of business respondents to the Technical Assistance Research Programs (TARP) Institute survey offered incentives for complaint-handling personnel to provide good customer service. The most common types of complaints from two separate TARP surveys concerned automobile problems, home improvements, mail-order purchases, and landlord-tenant disputes. (212, pp. 5–6)

Customer Service

Fallacy: American consumers care more about getting the lowest price than they care about quality.

Fact: According to a Yankelovich Clancy Shulman poll taken in the spring of 1990, Americans rank quality components in this order: reliability, durability, easy maintenance, ease of use, a known or trusted brand name, and, finally, a *low price*. (200, p. 44)

Fallacy: Japanese consumers are the toughest in the world!

Fact: It depends on the product. When it comes to footwear, Germans are adamant about the footwear specifications and expect salespeople to prove a shoe's unique construction and materials will produce a shoe that performs as well as promised. It is true that Japanese consumers can be tough in some areas, such as automobiles. The least demanding auto owners are the Italians. Autos produced there have paint finishes and interior and exterior trim that Americans would reject out of hand.

What about American consumers? How tough are they? Again, it depends. Many think Americans are the toughest when it comes to cold cereals, perhaps because they have the largest selection. Since the English use very little makeup or fragrance, they're undemanding about those products. Americans are regarded as the toughest when it comes to cosmetics, since busy women demand value for their money.

Japanese prefer the thinnest drapes, Australians prefer thick drapes. Italians, Spaniards, and U.S. Hispanics are the toughest when it comes to laundry detergents, since they place great importance on the way their families look. In Germany, people complain if their newspaper is torn when delivered. Conclusion: There is no one toughest customer; it depends on the product or service offered. (200, p. 44)

 The average company loses about 20% of its customers every year. (354, p. 61)

Fallacy: It does not matter whether you get a new customer or keep an old one; a customer is a customer.

Fact: Ford Motor Company figures it costs *five times* as much to attract a new customer as to keep a present one. Reichheld and Susser note that keeping 5% more of their customers yields a 100% increase in profits. A normal company's growth rate can be doubled by cutting by half the number of lost customers each year. (4, p. 100)

1% IBM estimates that if it can improve customer satisfaction 1% among its AS/400 customers worldwide, it will gain more than $200 million over five years. (208, p. 102)

Fallacy: After numerous books, articles, and speeches during the 1980s about staying close to the customer, U.S. businesses have got this message.

Fact: Not unless you believe *one out of four* isn't too bad. That is the proportion of companies that regularly include customer expectations in the design of their new products and services. (82, p. 132)

Fallacy: In American business, "The customer is number 1."

Fact: When managers were asked if their organizations shared strategic information with customers, 33% said always or often. Likewise, when asked "Does your organization include customers on a product planning team," only 32% said always or often. When asked "Does your organization offer seminars or training programs for customers," only 40% said always or often. (13, pp. 151–164)

Fallacy: It's only American businesses that misunderstand their customers.

Fact: Foreigners *miss the mark too.* In 1960, Nissan started to test the U.S. market for Datsun (which means "running ahead fast" in Japanese). Americans were not impressed. True, the car was economical, but it was slow, hard to drive, low powered, and not very comfortable. In short, it lacked what American drivers expected. Nissan's U.S. representative kept telling Tokyo what Americans wanted, but the factory refused to believe American tastes were different from their own. After seven years Nissan finally delivered a product with pizzazz. The 240Z is still treasured by performance car buyers. (299, p. 20)

 Toyota made similar mistakes. In 1958 Toyota jumped into the American market with a low-performance, subcompact car. Three years later it had to drop out to redesign the little sedan. Toyota came back in 1964 with a better understanding of its foreign customer. (299, p. 20)

 IBM has an electronic customer support system that automatically diagnoses trouble and alerts service people who sometimes show up before users know they have a problem. (208, p. 100)

In Japan, taxi drivers often wear white gloves and spend spare moments shining their cabs. (374, p. 54).

National service competitions! Most Japanese banks engage in a nationwide competition every two years in which they are evaluated on their ability to handle three or four standard service problems. There are three levels of competition: one for those that do transactions; another for those that open accounts, process loans, and so on; and still another for supervisors. (374, p. 58)

■ Talk about consumer choice: Americans in 1989 could select from among 73 different hand soaps. (336, p. 1)

In 1992 North American customers had the opportunity to choose from among 650 different car and truck models compared to about 530 models 10 years earlier. (342, p. 72)

More to choose from: From 1979 to 1989, the number of major brands of toothpaste sold in the United States increased from 7 to 31. Producers offered the market 33 major brands of coffee in 1979. They offered 52 brands by 1989. Ford increased the number of car models it offered from 7 in 1960 to 28 in 1989. (109, p. 146)

Customer Demographics

 Where are the new customers coming from? The U.S. population grew to 250 million by 1990. Annual population growth averages 2% per year. Few business leaders would be satisfied with a sales growth rate of less than 2% a year, but most businesses face a pool of customers that is essentially stable. *More than half of this population growth* occurred in three states: California, Florida, and Texas. Eight other states accounted for one quarter of all the population growth: Georgia, Arizona, North Carolina, Virginia, Washington, Maryland, Colorado, and Nevada. The rest of the United States accounted for the remaining one-quarter of the population increase. (273)

 Consumer spending accounts for two-thirds of U.S. economic activity. (278)

■ Seventy-seven percent of all financial assets belong to those over 50. (4)

Fallacy: Social Security accounts for less of older Americans' incomes than do pensions.

Fact: Social Security accounts for 39% of older Americans' incomes, while pensions make up 17%. Those earning

$10,000–20,000 a year rely on Social Security for over 50% of their income. (181, pp. 17–18)

———

How much does the typical American household have to spend for gifts, entertainment, and eating out after paying for food, housing, utilities, and other basics? The answer is *$108 a month.* Yet, 11% of us say we don't have any money left after we pay for the basics. (291)

———

What two states enjoyed major gains in household income between 1988 and 1990? No, it wasn't California, or Texas, or Florida. While the income of the typical American family was dropping by 5% in those years, only New Mexico and Kentucky had a significant increase. The reason for Kentucky's increase was 13,000 new automotive manufacturing jobs with Toyota. New Mexico's increase also was due in part to new manufacturing jobs as well. (283)

———

Four out of every five Americans express general concern about threats to personal privacy. Some demographic groups are more concerned than others. Adults over 50 are the least concerned about privacy but hate target marketing where direct marketers use their name and addresses. Want another indicator of people's need for privacy? Between 1978 and 1990, the proportion of the population that did not apply for a job, credit, or insurance because it would require them to reveal personal information jumped from 14% to 30%. (274)

———

Fallacy: About 32% of Americans are African Americans, 21% Hispanic, and 18% Jewish.

Fact: According to a survey, that's what the typical American thinks is the correct percentage of minorities to the total U.S.

population. Actual figures for all minorities are considerably lower than what most people think. The true figures are 12% African American, 8% Hispanic, and less than 3% Jewish. (279)

By 1990, one in four Americans belonged to a racial or ethnic minority. What was the fastest-growing minority? The answer may surprise you. It was Asians and Pacific Islanders, who accounted for about 90% of the growth of "other races." Still they only account for 4 million people. Hispanics grew four times the national average to a total of 21 million. (275)

If the birth rates of Hispanics, African Americans, Asians, and other minorities remain stable, the United States will become a nation with no racial or ethnic majority around the year 2060. (286)

Couples (of all ages) without children make up the largest plurality of American households. (26) In 1970 married couples with children accounted for 41% of American households. In 1990 this group represented only 27%, and single parents and households made up of unrelated individuals rose dramatically from *29% to 44%*. The percentage of dual-earner couples with children remained the same in both 1970 and 1990, but "other kinds of married couples" and single-earner families with children dropped from *21% to 8%*. Married couples without children stayed at about 30%. One final note: The highest income of the various demographic groups is found among "empty nesters," married couples aged 45 to 64. These "empty nesters" represent only 13% of the population, but make 19% of the purchases. *In the United States childless households are in the majority.* (26; 287)

Thirty-eight percent of U.S. households have children, while 43% have pets (furry, feathered, or scaly). Estimates of the total number of pets range from 170 million to 210 million. Trivia: Americans don't trust people who don't have pets. Except for President Clinton we haven't elected a president since Woodrow Wilson who didn't have a dog (and the Clintons have a cat). (292)

Fallacy: It's the parents who take care of the kids.

Fact: Not always. The average woman can expect to spend more years caring for her mother than for her children. (333)

Research shows that more than 90% of the middle-aged adults who are caring for their parents are women. (333)

The number of baby boomers (born 1946 to 1964) is still increasing. How can that be, you may ask? Because boomers from other countries are migrating to the United States. The baby boomers should peak at 78 million in 1993 and remain the largest consumer group for the next 20 to 30 years. Today, one in three Americans is a baby boomer. (288)

Fallacy: Women may be the major buyers for food, clothing, and other items in the United States, but men buy far more new cars.

Fact: Women bought 49% of new cars in 1991, compared with only 36% in 1981, and the percentage is expected to continue rising. (195)

Economy

Fallacy: High-tech investments in our nation's infrastructure, such as bullet trains and optical fiber networks, will yield the greatest returns to our economy.

Fact: Repairing potholes in our streets yields higher returns. Cost-benefit analyses on individual projects show that the highest returns come from maintenance on our present stock of capital goods (up to 40%) and from highway projects to relieve traffic congestion in cities (returns of 10% to 20%). (449)

Fallacy: No community wants a nuclear waste dump site in its area.

Fact: Twenty U.S. communities applied to host nuclear dump sites by mid-1992. Sixteen of them were Indian reservations. (188)

Fallacy: The federal budget deficit in the United States represents a larger share of our nation's economy than ever before.

Fact: As of 1992, the U.S. government was in deficit in 35 of the past 40 years. The debt was about 55% of gross domestic product (GDP) when President Eisenhower was in office. It fell to 25% in fiscal 1974 and rose back to its 1950's level of 55% by fiscal 1992. (119, p. A16)

Where does the federal government spend its discretionary dollars? In 1992, the chances were one in three that a domestic discretionary dollar would be spent on the savings and loan bailout. (121)

The American economy is the "biggest." It was $5.2 trillion in 1990. That is 40% larger than the Japanese. It's the biggest market for both foreign goods and foreign capital. (383, p. 14)

A sure sign we were in a pretty bad recession in 1991: Worldwide sales of Rolls Royce cars were down 48%. (90) When times get hard, people must cut back somewhere!

Are we giving the economy a facelift? In 1992, $60 million of new tax revenue will come from eliminating the tax deduction for cosmetic surgery. (86)

Fallacy: The mortgage interest tax deduction we claim when we file our personal income tax returns mostly helps middle- and lower-income people.

Fact: Not since the 1986 tax revision, which raised the standard deduction and lowered marginal tax rates. Since then, the mortgage interest tax subsidy favors high-income people. (52) *One-half* of the benefits of this deduction went to households earning more than $75,000 in 1991. Only *one-tenth* of the benefits went to households earning less than $40,000. (188) The wealthiest 20% of American households get three times as much federal housing aid, mostly in tax subsidies, as the poorest 20% get in low-income housing expenditures. (190, p. 16)

———

Fallacy: Most Americans increased their wealth during the economic expansion of the 1980s.

Fact: One study shows that wealth increases were concentrated in the top 0.5% income group—a mere 500,000 households. Even more startling, the 5% income rise these few wealthy people enjoyed came mainly from conservative investments of inherited wealth, not from their work. (55)

———

 Spend now—save later. U.S. national savings was only 4% in the 1980s compared to nearly 21% in Japan. (403, p. 23)

———

Fallacy: The median household income in the United States is increasing.

Fact: Only when it is stated in current dollars. When it is adjusted for inflation, median family income in the United States has not changed since 1969. If you had the feeling you were not making progress, now you know you weren't. (89)

———

Fallacy: The United States, unlike Japan and other countries, has no industrial policy.

Fallacy: All industries are taxed the same.

———

Fact: Lester Thurow's work *The Zero-Sum Solution* challenges both these fallacies. He found that the effective tax rate varied among industries. For instance, the tax rate for the computer industry was 26%, railroads 8%, electronics 13%, and chemicals a *negative* 5%. The conclusion is that such an imbalance in tax rates shows the government's role in fostering or hindering industry. (400)

Predictions are that by 2010, Japan, which is about the size of Montana and has half the U.S. population, will have a bigger economy than America's. Consider the following trends:

∎ In 1960 their economy was 10% the size of America's; in 1992, it was just over 60%.

∎ Their trade surplus has doubled in seven years despite a 50% increase in the value of their currency.

∎ Their household saving rate is more than three times higher than America's. (339, p. 60)

═══

Who has the most buying power? Per capita GDP, when adjusted for purchasing power to show what consumers can afford, shows the United States has the most at $17,615. Who's next? No, it's not Japan. Canada, with $16,375, is 2nd, Norway is 3rd at $15,940, and *Japan is a distant 14th* with $13,135, just before Finland and right after Belgium. (352, p. 107) Conclusion: You can buy a lot more with your money here than you can in other countries.

═══

The U.S. national debt is growing, but so is our gross national product (GNP), the source of our ability to pay it. Our national debt is $3 trillion and rising. The 1990 interest on it topped $169 billion, or more than the entire federal budget until 1968. (39, p. 5) (But our GNP was less than $1 trillion in 1968, while it is over $5 trillion today.)

═══

Fallacy: The price of raw materials of many kinds continues to rise like the cost of most goods and services.

Fact: Not after you correct for inflation. Raw material prices in 1990 were 30% less than they were in 1980 and almost 40% less than they were in 1970. (100, p. 41)

Half the stock traded on the New York Stock Exchange is held by institutional investors, including pension funds, endowments, insurance companies, and mutual funds. (403, p. 24)

———

We used less steel in America in 1990 than we used in 1960, though our GNP was 2.5 times greater. (100, p. 41) No wonder the United States has gone through a major upheaval trying to adjust to its overcapacity in steel production!

———

GNP falls if a man marries his housekeeper. Her services become unpaid, and the national economy appears to be poorer. (47, p. 85)

———

 Fallacy: Today it does not make a great deal of economic difference whether a child is raised in a two- or one-parent family.

Fact: Nine of 10 children from an intact family avoid poverty. One of 2 children in female-headed households are poor. (6) Some time during the first 10 years of their lives, 73% of American children in single-parent families will be poor. This compares to 20% in two-parent families. There are 15 million American children growing up without fathers. In fact, the best predictor of crime in a community is the percentage of single-parent families with children between 12 and 20 years old. Almost 60% of American prisoners spent some time in the foster care system. (7)

———

 Concerned about the amount of federal money spent on welfare? Then consider this fact: The federal government spent *six times* as much on savings and loan and bank bailouts in 1991 as it spent on welfare. (42)

Since 1980, the federal government has spent 59% less on U.S. cities. (42)

Fallacy: With the cold war ended, we will cut defense spending significantly.

Fact: Of all former President Bush's proposed spending for the next five years, only 0.6% will come from Pentagon budget cuts. (86)

Fallacy: In his 1992 presidential campaign, Ross Perot stated that government officials financed long-term portions of the federal debt with short-term money to keep interest rates down. He described that as suicide.

Fact: Several noted economists have urged the Treasury to do what Mr. Perot claims they have done. They think that if the Treasury cut back long-term borrowing, it would help lower long-term interest rates. Despite these economists' advice, the Treasury has done little of this short-term financing of the federal debt. (285)

Fact: The $137 billion spent in 1991 for defense expenditures accounted for just 2.4% of U.S. gross domestic product. (122, p. 89)

Sign of the cold war's end? The Department of Defense planned to spend $1,000,000 on softballs in 1992. (Our fighting men need to keep their competitive edge!) (188)

Fallacy: The Gulf War cost the United States billions of dollars.

Fact: Assuming we are able to collect all the money owed, we made a profit! The Pentagon has admitted that the marginal cost of the war was $38 billion and the foreign contributions totaled $52 billion—so the United States actually turned a bit of a profit. It's called collective leadership. The United States leads and the United States collects—not bad business if you have a huge budget deficit. (377, p. 55)

━━━━━

Fallacy: The United States, which many consider to be the world's policeman, spends more of every tax dollar on weaponry and defense than does any other nation.

Fact: Guess again! Israel spends 20 cents of every dollar on defense—at least four times what the United States spends. (70, p. 52)

━━━━━

Fallacy: The establishment of the European Monetary System in 1979 marked the first effort to establish a common European currency.

Fact: The first European unified monetary system with a common currency was established around 800 A.D. during Charlemagne's rule. (44, pp. 40–41)

━━━━━

Preparing for the future? Forty-six percent of U.S. domestic spending goes to the elderly; only 11% goes to children. (90)

Economies of Foreign Countries

Fallacy: India remains a poor and technologically backward nation.

Fact: India enjoys the world's third largest scientific and technical work force, trailing only the United States and the former Soviet Union. Spending on consumer goods in India will rise 10% a year through the year 2000, according to an estimate from India's Planning Commission. (455, pp. 128, 130)

Fallacy: U.S. foreign aid to Israel has produced an economic powerhouse.

Fact: Not that you could notice! The United States has given Israel $15 billion of aid during the past 10 years. That amounts to 15 times more aid per capita than we gave to Egypt, the next largest recipient. Despite this support, Israel's 1989 growth rate was only 1.1%, while its rate of inflation was 21% and its unemployment rate was 9%. Israel owes $16.4 billion in foreign debt. (58, p. 253) It is one U.S. investment that has not yielded much of a return.

Fallacy: The breakup of the former Soviet Union greatly disperses economic power among the 15 resulting republics.

Fact: Power of all types will be dispersed, but the Republic of Russia—by far the largest republic—now has most of the power and resources. It has 51% of the population, 60% of industrial production, and 76% of the territory. It also may wind up with all the nuclear weapons. (58, p.78)

———

Just how hard did economic recession hit the former Soviet Union in 1990–1991? Consider these facts:

∎ Industrial production declined 20% in 1990 and 40% in 1991.

∎ Total gross national product fell 15% in 1991. That is a greater decline than the United States experienced during the Great Depression.

∎ Inflation exceeded 20% in 1990 and topped 100% in 1991 after a 300% rise in the money supply.

∎ Seventy-one million Soviets lived on $115 per month or less.

∎ The state budget deficit swelled to 10% of the GNP, which is more than twice the U.S. level. (58, p. 96)

———

Before the reunification of East and West Germany in October 1991, the 62 million people in West Germany had a per capita income of $20,440, while those in communist East Germany had a per capita income less than $5,000. (58, p. 115)

———

Fallacy: It is better to ease the newly liberated European countries into free market economics than to push change too quickly.

Fact: The example of Poland indicates that "shock therapy" may be better. Poland put macroeconomic changes into effect immediately and soon suffered 200% inflation while real income fell 40%. But free prices, restraint in tax and monetary policies, and a currency that enjoys international convertibility are turning the economy around. Gradual change in Yugoslavia, Hungary, and the former Soviet Union have made the pain of change last longer and produced fewer positive results. (58, pp. 131–132)

Fallacy: The United States realizes the importance of helping the newly liberated nations of Eastern Europe convert to free market economics and is doing as much as can be done to aid the process.

Fact: Are we doing all we can to help? In 1991, the city of Denver paid more to get a major league baseball team than the United States gave in aid to Poland. (58, pp. 132–133)

 The most successful developing countries are those in East Asia. Eight of the region's 23 countries have averaged a 5% annual economic growth rate, more than any West European country. The Pacific Rim accounts for 20% of the world economy. (58, p. 148)

Fallacy: The Pacific Rim countries are becoming economic powerhouses.

Fact: Not all of them, most notably Vietnam. It has a long way to go. Seven million people almost starved after poor harvests in the late 1980s. The country suffers a 20% unemployment rate as it tries to absorb 1 million new workers into the labor force each year. Sixty percent of the economy comes from trade with the former Soviet Union and Eastern Europe, and this trade recently fell sharply because of the weakness of those economies. Hanoi is having trouble paying the $18 billion debt it owes to Russia. To earn hard currency on the international market, Vietnam has resorted to selling old U.S. military equipment left behind as scrap metal. The Vietnamese have a per capita income of $130, making the country one of the five poorest on the planet. (58, pp. 259–260) These people who suffered in war also are suffering in peace even as they live among the dynamically growing Pacific Rim nations.

Fallacy: For a nation with the world's second largest economy, Japan does not pay its fair share to the United Nations.

Fact: Japan is the second largest contributor, both to the United Nations and to the International Monetary Fund. (58, p. 150)

Fallacy: Saudi Arabia has almost endless cash reserves.

Fact: The Saudis' cash reserves seem larger than they are because of the country's relatively small population. Actually, the entire Saudi gross national product of $82 billion is less than the U.S. government spends on Medicare in one year. (58, p. 213)

———

 Mexico's largest source of income is oil. Second are the *maquiladoras* (low-skill, low-pay plants near the U.S. border that produce products for foreigners). The proposed free trade zone would do away with these *maquiladoras* by abolishing the tariff structure that makes them possible. (11, p. 34)

———

Fallacy: All the new jobs going to Mexico will mean fewer illegal immigrants.

Fact: Mexico's fast-growing population increases its work force by 1 million each year. Many of these workers do not reach the eighth grade. Unemployment was 13.5% in the spring of 1991. This means that thousands of new jobs with U.S. companies would help little to stop the flow of immigrants into the United States. It also means that Mexican wages will not rise much in the near future. (11, p. 34)

Education and
Business

Fallacy: Machine capital is the most important factor in expanding American productivity throughout this century. (You'll never guess what was number one.)

Fact: Between 1929 and 1982, *education* prior to work was responsible for a 26% expansion of our productive capacity. Even more impressive, learning on the job accounted for about 55% of all the U.S. productive capacity. Machine capital did contribute a respectable 20%. (250)

Fallacy: U.S. growth primarily depends upon capital investment.

Fact: It may be hard to believe, but in large part it depends on investment in education. From 1948 to 1982 one-third of the nation's gain in gross national product came from the increase in the education level of the U.S. work force and about half the growth was the result of technological innovation and increased know-how (which also depends on education). These are the results of studies by Edward Dennison, an expert in growth economics. (264, p. 102)

Higher education in the United States is a $100 billion business, or about 2.7% of our gross national product. (242)

Fallacy: U.S. corporations that give financial support to schools continue to give almost exclusively to colleges and universities.

Fact: This trend is changing, as youngsters are beginning to get more help from corporations. In 1992, 65% of corporations said they gave to elementary schools and 36% supported preschool programs. These figures are up from 27% and 14%, respectively, in 1990. (456, p. 147)

At least 23 million Americans—about 20% of all adult Americans—cannot read this sentence. About 12 million more can read a little, but they cannot function well in today's economy. One-third of 360 companies responding to a recent survey said that they constantly reject job applicants because of poor reading and writing skills. Half the companies said that some of their employees have serious math and reading weaknesses. (142, p. 68)

Fallacy: Our poor educational system doesn't affect business.

Fact: The United States is losing $25 billion a year in productivity through inadequate education and training of the work force:

∎ We have 22 million functionally illiterate people.

∎ One million students per year never complete high school.

∎ About 750,000 who do graduate from high school each year *cannot* read their diplomas.

∎ Private industry spends $40 billion annually for remedial training in reading, writing, and computational skills. (332)

Fallacy: U.S. industrial firms must take what they get in employee basic education skills from our education system.

Fact: Many of them spend a lot to upgrade their employees' basic educational skills. The Big Three auto companies are an example.

By the end of 1992, General Motors officials estimate that 30,000 workers will have studied in the firm's basic education program at a cost of $30 million. Ford Motor Company invests $50–60 million a year in its education programs. About 31,400 workers have participated. Between 3,000 and 4,000 Chrysler workers have studied in the firm's basic education program as of mid-1992. (81, p. B1)

 How weak are the skills of the American work force? The U.S. Office of Technology assessment and other investigators believe that 20–30% of U.S. workers do not have the basic skills they need to perform their current jobs, to participate well in training programs, or to implement new technology well. A 1986 survey of adults aged 21 to 25 taken by the National Assessment of Educational Progress showed that 20% of the respondents *could not read at the eighth-grade level.* (117, p. 48)

 In a recent survey, only 12% of U.S. employers think that high school graduates write well and 22% think they have mastered math. (172, p. 70)

Fallacy: Most employers care about the academic performance of the high school graduates they hire.

Fact: According to the National Center on Education and the Economy, *98% of employers do not* review their high school applicants' transcripts because they think their course work is not relevant to the work they will do if hired. (143, p. 66)

All Japanese high school graduates will have taken six years of English language classes. (86)

American public and private elementary and secondary schools currently serve 40 million students, and it costs $150 billion annually for them to operate. (248, p. 9)

In 1945, 6- to 14-year-old children had an average of 25,000 words in their written vocabulary. Now they have an average of 10,000. Four of the six best-selling, extracurricular books in college bookstores in 1990 were collections of cartoons. In 1990, only 40% of Americans under the age of 30 said they read a daily newspaper, while 65% of those older than 50 said they did. (88)

According to the National Education Goals Panel, only 18% of U.S. eighth graders can solve problems with decimals, fractions, and proportions; classify geometric figures; read; interpret and construct line and circle graphs; and translate verbal problems into simple algebraic expressions. (251)

In recent studies of math proficiency, U.S. 12th graders scored 12th or below among students from 15 countries in geometry, advanced algebra, and calculus. U.S. high school seniors also ranked 9th in physics, 11th in chemistry, and 13th in biology out of 17 countries. (261, p. 3) But the kids think they are doing okay. When asked, 68% of them thought they were "good in math." (258, p. 115)

As the comedian said, "I get no respect." Gallup asked respondents to rank the goals set out in America 2000 (President Bush's Education Program). Respondents rated making U.S. students first in the world in math and science as *the least important.* (258, p. 118)

Fallacy: Educational reform is seen as a high priority by American parents.

Fact: False. According to one study, "American parents appeared to be no more likely in 1990 and 1991 than they were in 1980 to believe there was an urgent need for educational reform. Instead, American parents seemed pleased with the education their children were receiving." (429)

 One-third of American 17-year-olds cannot identify which countries the United States fought against in World War II. (260, p. 31)

 The U.S. high school dropout rate is roughly 25%. (263, p. 143) (However, some will, as will be seen shortly, eventually get their high school degree.)

Fallacy: High school dropouts are becoming a serious problem in the United States.

Fact: It depends on your standard, but as of October 1985, 86.5% of whites, 87.5% of African Americans, and 70% of Hispanics received a high school education. Overall, 86% of young people between the ages of 25 and 29 were high school graduates (twice the percentage for 1940). The lesson to learn from this fact is that while we may have a larger percentage getting high school diplomas today than in 1940, most graduates appear to be poorly educated. (248, p. 10)

 Only 60 cents of every education dollar makes it to the classroom. Forty cents goes to capital spending, maintenance, and, most noteworthy, the board of education. Between 1980 and 1990, administrative costs for U.S. schools have climbed nearly twice as fast as spending on teachers. (263, p. 148)

Fallacy: *A voucher system* that allows students to attend any public school they choose in their state *will cause massive enrollment shifts.*

Fact: So far, we only have a few locations where students have this choice. One is Minnesota, where such a plan has been in effect since 1988. By mid-1992, only 1% of the state's students had switched schools. (172, p. 74)

Fallacy: Far fewer African Americans than whites graduate from U.S. secondary schools.

Fact: True 20 years ago when the school dropout rate of African-American children was 57% higher than for white children. But, today, African-American males and females graduate from high school at roughly the same rate as do their white counterparts. (76, p. 42)

 African Americans' literacy rates are up, too, for those who stay in school. About 97% of African-American high school students read at a minimum literacy level or higher—nearly the same percentage as for white students, and up from an 82% rate for African Americans in 1971. (76, p. 42)

 Teaching them how to walk and talk? Management of Super Value Stores Food Club market in Denver found that it has to teach its workers how to smile and walk erect; it even has to ask some to come to work with their shoes tied and shirts ironed! (354, p. 59)

Half of all new teachers leave the teaching field within seven years. Also, America may need to replace *1 million teachers,* half the current work force, by the year 2000 because of retirement and natural attrition. (268)

Fallacy: Spending more money per student in our public schools will better prepare students for college.

Fact: So far this hasn't worked. Since 1970, per student spending rose 427%, while average Scholastic Aptitude Test (SAT) scores fell 49 points. (161)

Fallacy: You can't just throw money at education and expect it to improve!

Fact: Try throwing some money *(and respect)* at teachers and see what happens! In Japan teachers have high status and respect. Most come from the top third of college graduates. *Their beginning salaries are higher than those of engineers.* In Germany, secondary teachers' salaries are similar to those of judges and doctors employed by the government. Teaching in the United States does not enjoy the same status or salary. (425, p. 4)

 The United States is not the only one concerned about the quality of graduates entering the work force. In a European study, *84%* of employers think business schools are not flexible enough, and *72%* said their needs are not being met by high school graduates. Many of these businesses are establishing their own graduate training programs, often with a consortium of other companies. (394)

 Japan and Sweden allocate comparable resources to all schools. In the United States local annual per student funding ranges from about *$2,000 to $6,000* and teachers' salaries vary widely by state and local area. Japan provides uniform teacher salaries and per capita school funding so poorer areas are on par with affluent ones. Sweden provides extra resources to needy schools such as those in remote rural areas. (425, p. 4)

Almost all Japanese high school students get jobs through school recommendations to employers. Most German noncollege youth enter an apprenticeship program. The U.S. educational system has no such system, and students receive inadequate preparation for employment.

 As just noted, Japanese noncollege-bound youth get jobs *almost exclusively* through school-employer linkages. Almost all high school students seeking work are placed in jobs through their schools, which act as agents of the public employment service. Each high school has ties with employers who assign a certain number of jobs to the school for its graduates. Most prestigious employers with better job offers recruit from higher-ranked schools. Japanese employers usually base hiring decisions on school recommendations, which are based on students' grades and "behavior" (e.g., attendance records).

In Sweden, by age 15, students have completed 6 to 10 weeks of work orientation. Students choosing a vocational field are typically trained in school but also have practical training with an employer.

In Germany, all noncollege-bound youth begin apprenticeships at age 15 or 16, and training usually lasts three years. Youth typically spend one to two days a week studying in vocational schools and the rest of the week receiving on-the-job training from employers. (425, p. 5)

Here are some facts about vocational education. More girls than boys are enrolled; more rural than urban students are enrolled. Parents of vocational students have considerably lower incomes than do those of college-bound students, and proportionally more vocational students belong to minority groups. (253)

Fallacy: Apprenticeship programs are for "high schoolers" and other youth.

Fact: The average age of U.S. apprentices is 29. In the U.S. apprenticeship is not widely used nor is it generally a program for youth. Apprentices in the United States constitute less than 0.3% of the labor force. (365, pp. 2–11)

———

 About 430,000 high school juniors and seniors (8% of the total) participated in cooperative education (co-op) programs in the 1989–90 school year. Enrollment was concentrated in marketing (primarily in retail and trade), trade and industry (includes auto mechanics and auto body), and business (carpentry and construction business placements are typically clerical and secretarial). Co-op students account for less than 4% of high school students in all four grades, although 50% of high school students will never attend college. (365, p. 16)

———

Fallacy: Co-op education in high schools is for poor kids.

Fact: Forty-one percent of co-op participants come from the upper half of the socioeconomic distribution. (365, p. 18)

———

Fallacy: By the year 2000, one will need a college degree to get just about any job.

Fact: Most won't. Seventy percent of jobs at the turn of the century will not require a baccalaureate degree. (38, p. 69)

———

 However, we still need college graduates. According to demographic projections, an increasing number of jobs will require college degrees in the 1990s and beyond, yet the number of people with the qualifications to fill these positions is expected to decline. (362, p. 2)

In the United States there are 156 universities and 1,853 colleges with a total enrollment of almost 8 million. These institutions spend about $80 billion yearly, or about $13,000 per student. (248, p. 10)

Students in Florida state colleges are required to complete 24,000 words of writing before their junior year. (161)

Five percent of bachelor's degrees awarded by American colleges and universities go to foreign students, and 10% of the master's degrees and 20% of doctoral degrees go to foreign students. Most amazing, at the doctoral level, 30% of the business and management, 42% of the mathematical, and 51% of the engineering degrees are earned by foreign students. (261, p. 4)

Foreign invasion? Almost 37,000 Japanese students enrolled in U.S. colleges in 1990–91, but that is second to 39,600 Chinese students who enrolled. All told, in 1991, the number of foreign students rose 5.3% to a total of 407,529. What was the most popular subject? Over 19% chose business management, followed closely by engineering, at 18%. (254)

As of early 1992, 43% of the members of Taiwan's cabinet held Ph.D.s from American universities. No members of the U.S. cabinet that year held a Ph.D. from anywhere. (90) A politician would call that a very favorable balance of trade in Ph.D. degrees.

Catching up—slowly. One researcher figures that if present trends continue, it will be 2,000 more years until women earn as many doctoral degrees in math each year as men earn. (176)

▪ *Non-Asian* minorities represent only 10% of enrollment in U.S. engineering programs. (413)

Women represent only 16% of U.S. students in engineering programs. (413)

In the past 30 years the number of 22-year-olds acquiring bachelor's degrees in science and engineering remained at around 4%. If that trend continues, there will be a shortfall of more than 400,000 science and engineering B.A.s through the year 2000. The country already expects to have a shortage of 27,000 Ph.D.s by the year 2000. (265)

▪ In 1992, there were 436,000 African-American men in college, but 609,000 of them in prison. (80, p. 144)

In 1979, 9.5% of employed African-American men holding a *college degree* earned poverty-level pay. In 1991, that percentage had risen to 14.8%. (89)

Say it ain't so! If an extra 10% of university students majored in engineering, the growth rate of the economy *would rise by 0.5%* a year. By contrast, if law school enrollment doubled, the growth rate *would fall by 0.3%* annually. (237, p. 74)

The customer is always right. In search of greater relevance, many companies are collaborating with business schools to create custom programs for their business. Such collaborating is growing at a 25% clip per year. (256)

Fallacy: "I don't need no education!"

Fact: Education makes a lot of difference in pay. In 1987 in the United States, a male high school graduate averaged an inflation-adjusted salary of $27,733. Such a person would have earned $31,667 in 1973. During this 14-year period, the pay of a male without a high school education fell from $19,562 to $16,094. This means a decline in inflation-adjusted pay of 18%. A male with a college education would have increased his pay from $49,531 to $50,115. A typical male college graduate was earning about 80% more than his high school counterpart in 1980. The gap between them almost doubled by 1990. Japanese high school graduates' pay, by contrast, rose 13% between 1979 and 1987. (1, pp. 205–206)

The more education you have, the more money you make. A recent study by University of Michigan professors John Bound and George Johnson shows that this relationship existed earlier, but was hidden by the high number of college students during the war in Vietnam. Not all of them could find appropriate jobs when they entered the work force during the 1970s. Far fewer graduates were looking for jobs (and finding them) during the 1980s. This opened the pay spread between high school and college graduates by 15%. According to this study, the underlying trend of higher income for higher education has probably been pretty stable for 100 years. (75)

Maybe there is no such thing as a free lunch, but education comes pretty close to it. On average, learning in school and on the job accounts for about half of the difference in what people earn in the United States. Career, location choices, chance, and opportunity account for the other half. (249)

■ Return on investment for an MBA degree is slowing down. Columbia University Business School compared its graduates' average starting salaries over two decades with their annual tuition. In 1978, this ratio was 6.3 ($12,600 starting salary divided by $2,000 in tuition). In 1991, it was 3.25 ($53,000/$16,300). (399)

Educators have known for years that family income is the best predictor of a child's success in school. Average combined SAT scores offer evidence of this relationship. Scores of children from families with annual income above $70,000 average 997; scores of those whose annual family income is less than $10,000 average 768. (86)

Fallacy: Corporate giving to schools in America is growing and will help improve poor, inner-city public schools.

Fact: During the 1970s, corporate giving to schools showed average annual increases of 15%. By 1987, that figure was 5.1%, and by 1988, 2.4%. Corporations donated most of this to colleges and universities, especially prestigious ones. Primary and secondary schools received only *1.5%* of corporate gifts in 1989. (1, pp. 280–281)

80% Now the good news. In a survey by the U.S. General Accounting Office (GAO), about 80% of survey respondents from large companies plan to cultivate ties with schools to help improve the quality of potential future employees. (362, p. 9)

 Americans spent $500 million on business books in 1991. (154) (This fact had nothing to do with our deciding to write this book in 1992; we were motivated only by the opportunity to serve you, the reader.)

Employee Compensation

Fallacy: U.S. workers are paid more than workers in other parts of the world.

Fact: U.S. hourly labor costs are among the lowest in the industrial world. (237, p. 75)

———

This is progress? Real GNP in the United States rose 28% from 1973 to 1990. But, during this time, real hourly wages of nonsupervisory workers fell 12% and their real weekly wages declined 18%. Weekly wages fell more because some employers changed to part-time workers to whom they did not have to pay fringe benefits. (100, p. 53)

———

Fallacy: Average U.S. work force salaries are increasing.

Fact: From 1973 to 1989 the average U.S. salary in real dollars fell about 25% because more Americans work in fast-food restaurants than in manufacturing. (303)

———

Fallacy: Pay is low for people in food preparation work.

Fact: If low pay in food preparation work is your problem, then why don't you learn to slice lox (smoked salmon) and get a job at Zabar's delicatessen in New York City? It would be an excellent career move. Lox slicers with 10 years or more experience earn an average of $60,000 a year at Zabar's. (188)

 Real wages (wages adjusted for inflation) of non-supervisory workers in the United States fell 12% between 1975 and 1992. This puts these nonsupervisory personnel where they were in the late 1950s. (162, p. 26)

Fallacy: Most of the jobs created in the United States from 1979–1990 pay the minimum wage. (This fact was asserted by Ross Perot during his 1992 presidential campaign.)

Fact: Most of these jobs pay above the minimum wage. Almost 60% of them pay over $6.10 an hour. Maybe $6.10 *is* minimum wage to Ross. (285)

Talk about a compensation gap! It would take 44,492 years for a Nike worker in Indonesia to earn Michael Jordan's former endorsement fee for the shoes that worker makes. (148)

Fallacy: Workers are never satisfied with their pay, or with the pay that others make compared with theirs.

Fact: The management consulting firm Sirota Alper and Pfan randomly surveyed 350 employees in a national sample. It is true that two-thirds thought CEOs got too big a share of corporate profits, but nearly half believed their share was about right, and a solid majority believed stockholders' share was about right. (233, p. 62)

 Everybody knows that top executives get much of their pay in stock options and other flexible forms. What about lower-level workers? Japanese workers get an average of about 25% of their pay as a flexible bonus. The average is only 1% in the United States. (40, p. 51)

Fallacy: Workers know that good pay comes from good work performance.

Fact: A survey of 845 blue- and white-collar workers showed that 45% of them saw no link between performance and pay. (40, p. 51)

 The actual pay of American and Japanese workers is relatively close, but we get more bang for our bucks. The hourly compensation cost for production workers in manufacturing, in 1990 dollars, using purchasing power as a gauge, shows that U.S. workers are in the best shape. The U.S. workers' $14.77 hourly wage compares to Western Germany's $14.67 wage. The United Kingdom's $10.60 and Japan's $9.22 wages are far behind. (358, p. 61)

Concerned about your pay? Consider that 700 million people in the world today earn no more than $2.50 a day. (91)

Fallacy: The closing of several General Motors (GM) plants in 1991 and 1992 means GM no longer has to pay the workers from those plants.

Fact: Hardly. GM's contract with the United Auto Workers states that after GM workers have been laid off for 36 weeks, they get full wages from a Jobs Bank funded by GM. That Jobs Bank has paid out $1.7 billion since October 1990. The fund was expected to be depleted by January 1993, but GM still must pay part of their workers' unemployment benefits, which amounts to 95% of regular pay. (160)

Employee Involvement

Fallacy: In America, workers feel free to speak their mind.

Fact: According to the American Quality Foundation, a New York think tank, 70% of American workers are afraid to speak up with suggestions or to ask for clarification. (205, p. 38)

Fallacy: Introducing a quality program at work means a business is making better use of its employees.

Fact: Thirty-six percent of employees who reported to the Gallup Organization that their companies have quality programs say they do not participate in these activities. What causes over one-third of a business's human resources to sit idle? Major reasons given for not participating include a lack of available programs, not enough time to participate, irrelevant programs, and not being invited to participate! (306)

According to an article in *The Executive,* the typical *U.S. leading edge company has 2.3 suggestions per employee, per year.* Some Japanese companies have extraordinary employee involvement. Toyota averages 47.6 per employee, and Mazda's 126.5 is almost too high to believe. Canon averages 78.1 and Matsushita averages 79.6, both respectable averages, but one Japanese company, Tohoku Oki, tops the list with an astonishing *833.2 suggestions per employee per year.* (341, p. 32)

Fallacy: Employee stock ownership plans improve productivity and profits for a company.

Fact: According to the GAO, these plans *have not* (1) improved the productivity or profitability of sponsoring companies or (2) led to a high degree of employee control over or participation in corporate management. (366, p. 3)

━━━

Fallacy: *Japanese* autoworkers are a happy and contented lot.

Fact: The Confederation of Japan Auto Workers surveyed 10,000 of its 750,000 members and found that 86% complained of increased production quotas, a decrease in the number of factory workers, and compensatory overtime. When asked in 1990 about job satisfaction, 56% of the men and 36% of the women said they were satisfied. That is down from 70% for men and 46% for women in 1986. (388)

Environment and Business

Fallacy: The environment and concern for pollution costs jobs.

Fact: It creates some too. An analysis of 1988 U.S. pollution control shows that the industry supported nearly 3 million direct and indirect jobs. Some 2.5% of U.S. jobs are now in pollution control, almost all created since 1970. (430)

Need to practice what they preach? The Rio Earth Summit in June 1992 generated *7 tons* of trash per day. (148)

It's not my fault! While 83% of U.S. corporate executives believe that causing damage to the environment is a serious crime, only 49% believe that they should be held personally responsible for such an offense. (319)

It's a different story for the public. While 84% of the U.S. public also felt causing damage to the environment was a serious crime, they differed dramatically with those executives about accountability. In 75% of the cases, the public felt *executives should be held personally responsible.* (319)

Most Americans say they would replace 8 of 17 types of product packaging for the sake of the environment. What's the first packaging to go? Styrofoam boxes, followed by aerosol cans. What do Americans think is most wasteful? Sixty-seven percent think fast-food packaging is wasteful, 60% say toy packaging, and 56% say hair spray packaging. (276)

Fallacy: Plastic products cannot be recycled.

Fact: Some can and some cannot be recycled. Plastic lawn bags will not degrade, and they account for over 10% of the solid waste being added to landfills. But recycled plastics now make up 20–30% of the contents of new products. And you may repurchase that Kodak Fun-Saver® disposable camera you tossed. Kodak pays photo finishers to return used Fun-Savers to them because 86% of the camera's parts can be recycled and reused. (194, p. 19)

Fast-developing sales: The hottest photographic product in the early 1990s is the disposable camera. Sales of these little throwaway plastic cameras with plastic lenses rose 50% in 1991 and was estimated to become a $200 million market in 1992. (170)

Fallacy: Environmentalists are a few "nuts" running around trying to save the rain forest.

Fact: A *Wall Street Journal*/NBC News Poll released in August 1991 showed that 8 of 10 Americans considered themselves to be environmentally sensitive. (351, p. 34)

It's a green group out there. *Eighty percent* of Americans consider protecting the environment more important than keeping prices down. A smaller amount, 46%, said they have bought prod-

ucts based on a manufacturer's or product's environmental repu-
tation, and 53% said they have avoided products because of environmental concerns. (277)

In the United States, 80% of shoppers polled in 1989 said that protecting the environment was so important as to warrant *any cost.*
Only 15% disagreed. Eight years earlier, percentages agreeing and
disagreeing split evenly, at 40% and 40%. (405)

More important than safe sex? According to a Roper Poll, when
Americans were asked what they believe is important in the
1990s, 85% of them said the environment is the most serious
issue. The concern for the environment was followed by patrio-
tism and safe sex. (351, p. 34)

I think I understand! In 1990, 23% of Americans
claimed to have a clear understanding of acid rain,
but when asked to describe "the primary cause of
acid rain," only 6% could provide a minimal scientific explanation and an additional 10% were able
to provide general statements such as "smoke-
stacks" and "plants that burn coal." A majority of Americans
could not describe the cause of acid rain in any way. (338, p. 63)

Fallacy: Acid rain is a major health threat.

Fact: Not according to most scientists. They say
that acid rain is just a minor threat to rivers and
lakes and is not a serious threat to humans. (196, p.
98)

Fallacy: The United States imposes stricter industrial air pollution standards than those found in Europe.

Fact: A U.S. factory legally can emit *four times* the amount of air
pollution that a German plant can. (46)

CO₂ As the largest producer of carbon dioxide gas, expect American companies to face increased international pressure to reduce their emissions. Consider this fact: Since the beginning of the industrial revolution, the level of carbon dioxide has increased about 25% and is approaching the *maximum* amount that scientists believe has occurred naturally over the past *million years*. Carbon dioxide is responsible for about half the contribution greenhouse gases make to global warming. (419, p. 2)

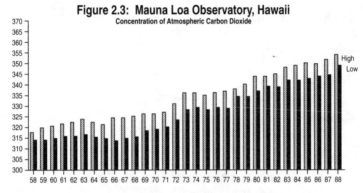

Figure 2.3: Mauna Loa Observatory, Hawaii
Concentration of Atmospheric Carbon Dioxide

Source: General Accounting Office

Fallacy: Americans are more concerned about the environment than are people in other nations.

Fact: It is close, but according to a survey by *Harvard Business Review*, Germans are more concerned, and we are tied with the Japanese and South Koreans. The Germans are also more concerned about education than we are—but it is close. Relatively speaking, the Japanese are nearly as concerned about their education system as we or the Germans are. (13, pp. 158–159)

∎ Who is most concerned about unemployment? Well, the Germans are, but surprisingly it is the South Koreans' main concern, even more so than the environment or education. (13, pp. 158–159)

∎ While everybody is somewhat concerned about alcohol and drugs, the Japanese are far less concerned about it than any other industrialized country. (13, pp. 158–159)

In 1990, a survey in the European Community (EC) showed that concern for the environment outranks unemployment as the most immediate and urgent problem. (404)

Consumers in Europe are paying a premium for goods that are recycled, recyclable, and nondamaging to the environment. Those willing to pay for environmentally friendly products pay a premium ranging from 50% in France to 80% in Germany. (405)

In a poll of 200 international corporate leaders by McKinsey and Company, 90% said the environmental challenge will be a central issue of the twentieth century, and they anticipate environmental expenditures increasing over the next decade by 50% to 100%, reaching a total of 3–6% of their firms' total revenues. (406)

Even in Eastern Europe, the environment is important. A poll taken in Czechoslovakia in early 1990 found that 83% of respondents considered improving environmental conditions to be the country's top priority. (410, p. 28)

What is your image of *hell on earth?* In Romania's small town of Copsa Mica, every person and object is covered in a film of black soot from a nearby plant that produces black powder, an ingredient used in the manufacture of rubber. Trees and bushes are black, the grass is stained, and everything looks like it has been dipped in ink. (410, p. 33)

 In Czechoslovakia, a dump with 3,500 tons of toxic waste containing nerve gas was discovered near Karlovyvary, the location of a spa famous for its mineral water hot springs. (410, p. 34)

 Black Sea or Dead Sea? The Black Sea receives 4,300 tons of nitrogen compounds, 900 tons of petroleum products, 600 tons of lead, and 200 tons of detergents from industrial waste per year. (410, p. 34)

 Can you imagine how much is still out there? Environmental Protection Agency Administrator William Reilly said the Clean Air Act of 1990 will remove 56 billion pounds of pollution each year from the air we breathe. That is *224 pounds of pollutants* for every woman, man, and child in America! (351, p. 34)

 The EPA estimates that $160 billion, or nearly *3% of the nation's GNP,* will be spent on pollution control by the year 2000. Many believe this to be a conservative estimate. Consider the following fallacy. (350, p. 21)

Fallacy: Federal regulations for the environment as well as personal health and safety in the workplace may be a hassle for the businesspeople who must abide by them, but the actual cost of these regulations to our economy is not so great.

Fact: The most widely accepted estimate of the cost of these regulations for 1991 is over a *half-trillion dollars,* or about 10% of that year's gross domestic product! (197, p. 94)

———

Fallacy: The United States has made a significant commitment to having clean air.

Fact: Not when you look closer. We will spend $25 billion a year for this purpose, which amounts to 24 cents a day per person. When you compare that to the 63 cents per person a day our people spend on alcoholic beverages and 43 cents for cigarettes, it doesn't seem like such a large sum. (196, p. 98)

———

Fallacy: No matter the cost, we need regulations that eliminate any known environmental, consumer, or occupational cancer hazard.

Fact: Nearly complete elimination has been the thinking since the Delaney Amendment passed in 1957. But one widely accepted study found that pollution, contaminants in the workplace, food additives, and medications account for less than 9% of cancer deaths. By contrast, smoking and poor diet cause almost two-thirds of fatal cancers. (197, p. 95)

———

Fallacy: American business isn't concerned about the environment and environmental issues.

Fact: At the 1990 annual meeting of the World Economic Forum, 650 industrial and governmental leaders ranked the environment as the number one challenge facing business. (348, p. 4)

Some other indicators that the environment is a factor in business decisions include the following:

∎ DuPont is getting out of a $750-million-a-year business because it may harm the earth's atmosphere. (349)

∎ Polaroid Corporation and Monsanto, among others, have started programs to raise employee participation in pollution control programs. (349)

▪ In August 1990, McDonald's and the Environmental Defense Fund formed a task force for reducing and recycling waste at McDonald's 11,000 restaurants. (349)

―――

Fallacy: Manufacturers raise their unit costs of production when they adopt more environmentally clean production methods.

Fact: *Cleaner production can save money.* One goal of the 3M Corporation is to lower air and water emissions 90% and solid waste 50% from 1990 levels. If successful, the company chairman estimates 3M will cut the inflation-adjusted unit cost of most products by 10%. Monsanto, DuPont, AT&T, and 3M plan to move toward closed-loop production that emits no discharges! (51, p. 74)

―――

Fallacy: There is not much more we can do to protect the environment unless we deindustrialize.

Fact: Those in the U.S. Office of Technology Assessment think we could cut industrial waste in the United States by 75% if we used advanced technologies. Also, studies by U.N. agencies report that industrialized countries could recycle more than 50% of their paper, glass, plastics, and metals if they had the proper infrastructure to do so. (50, p. 70)

―――

Fallacy: Global energy demands can only increase as people use more and more electrical appliances.

Fact: Not if we are smart. The Worldwide Energy Conference does project a 75% increase in global energy demand by the year 2020. But the newest lighting fixtures, air conditioners, furnaces, and refrigerators are from 50% to several times more efficient energy users than older models. The International Energy Agency in Paris estimates that industrial countries could cut energy demand by 20% by the year 2000 by using more energy-efficient equipment. Others estimate that in years to come, solar power could provide 30% of needed energy. (50, p. 70)

∎ Is *every* computer user a "power user"? Desktop computers use about 5% of the electricity consumed in the United States. The Environmental Protection Agency (EPA) estimates that an office desktop computer consumes around $100 of electricity per year, which is the amount needed to power for one month a house not heated by electricity or cooled by air conditioning. But help may be on the way. Intel Corporation engineers think that it's possible to build a desktop machine that can run continuously while consuming only 2% of the energy that today's desktops use. (32)

Fallacy: Global warming is the major environmental threat to the earth's inhabitants.

Fact: Global warming is certainly not the most immediate threat, nor is it the most difficult one with which to deal. According to a report from the World Bank, 2 million people, most of them children, die each year from *polluted water.* Solving this problem involves sanitation methods well known in developed countries. (101)

Fallacy: The Potomac is the most polluted river in the United States.

Fact: The most polluted river in the United States is the Rio Grande. Workers at chemical plants dump huge amounts of chemical waste into it between El Paso and the Gulf of Mexico. (11, p. 33)

 One type of water pollution is called "nonpoint" or diffuse sources of pollution (as opposed to pollutants discharged from a single specific "point.") Nonpoint pollution comes from a variety of land uses, including timber harvesting, urban runoff, land disposal, milling, agriculture, and construction. Guess which of these sources accounts for 50–70% of this pollution? It's *agriculture,* which includes soil erosion, overgrazing, and runoff from pesticides. (363, p. 2)

G-7 The "Greenhouse Seven" nations, including the United States and Japan, produce 45% of the world's greenhouse gases. Industrial nations contain 25% of the world's population and consume 70% of its resources. The richest 20% of people in the world have 150 times the income of the poorest 20%. (50, p. 69)

Fallacy: The United States does at least as well as other developed nations at recycling solid materials.

Fact: The *United States ranks last* among Office for Economic Cooperation and Development nations in recycling glass and 15th in paper. Germany and Japan reuse three times as much of their overall waste as does the United States. To give you one example of German effort, BMW makes plastics for its new cars from junked BMWs. BMW plans to be able to recycle 90% of each new car by 1997. (196, p. 100)

We're #1. The United States ranks number one in *garbage production.* The average citizen throws out 719 kilos of waste per person per year, which is about 20 times the weight of a typical American. The average Japanese throws out 337 kilos, and in Europe it's more like 300 kilos. (407)

Fallacy: The stream of garbage collection going to municipal trash collections will slow because the EPA set a goal to reduce it.

Fact: In 1988, the EPA set a goal to cut the total waste stream 25% by 1992. The result? The amount of *waste increased* 13% between 1988 and 1992. (196, p. 100)

Talk about killing trees! Equitable Life Assurance Society set a new world record for a single printing with 2.5 million copies of a 349-page document asking policyholders to vote on whether to demutualize the company and turn it into a public corporation. If you stacked these documents on top of each other, they would reach 104,166 feet, or about 20 miles high. That is more than 3–1/2 times the height of Mount Everest. (398)

Fallacy: Developed nations ruin their environments more than do the developing nations.

Fact: Developing countries tend to be worse environmental offenders. They often feel the need to exploit their natural resources to relieve their relative poverty. For example, while many people are concerned about rapid cutting of the Amazon rain forest, the northeastern United States and parts of northern Europe are more heavily forested now than they were 100 or 200 years ago, despite the effects of acid rain. (151, p. 86)

Fallacy: Tropical forests are being cut because they are worth more money cut than standing.

Fact: That may be the reason the developers cutting them down give, but it does not square with the facts. Converting a Brazilian forest to pasture produces about 220 pounds of meat per acre. But left standing, that forest can produce 2,750 pounds of food. Also, the value of fruits, nuts, and other products harvested each year from the standing forest can be twice the one-time revenue from logging. (50, p. 70)

 Fallacy: Destruction of tropical forests is not really a significant ecological problem.

Fact: The forests absorb much of the poisonous carbon dioxide (CO_2) in the air. The level of CO_2 in the air has risen 20% in the last century. (50, p. 70)

To pay off huge national debts, many developing countries are selling off the precious resources they will need to industrialize during the years ahead. Thirty-three countries exported tropical timber in 1985. Twenty-three of them likely will exhaust their supplies during the next decade. If they industrialize without the cleaner technology these resources could provide, they will increase global pollution. (50, p. 69)

Fallacy: Food output is rising in developing nations, giving us a chance to defeat world hunger.

Fact: Food output is rising, but not the amount of food per person. One major problem is that several forces have degraded 11% of the world's land. That is an area bigger than China and India combined. (50, p. 69)

Ethics

 At the trial of a lawsuit brought against Ford over the Pinto's safety, the prosecution introduced a Ford study showing that a committee of managers and designers estimated that the placement of the fuel tank would cause 180 burn deaths, and 2,100 burned vehicles that would cost Ford a total of *$49.5 million* in court judgments for negligent design. This was balanced against the cost to rectify the design for 100 million cars and 1.5 million light trucks with the Pinto-like gas tank design. Such a design change would cost *$11* each, for a total expenditure of *$137 million*. Management decision was a straightforward business decision to pay the less costly probable judgments for the burn deaths and keep the design the same. (367, p. 10)

Fallacy: In the wake of ethical scandals in business during the 1980s, young adults will take more care to observe ethical practices as they advance their careers.

Fact: Let's hope so; however, many young adults seem to have learned a different lesson from the 1980s. An astonishing 37% of Americans in their twenties say that corruption is important in getting ahead! (188)(130)

Fallacy: Businesspeople have no ethics, integrity, or social vision.

Fact: Some may not, but many do. The Business Enterprise Trust presenting its first annual awards recognized those whose acts noted merit. Among the first winners were

∎ Merck & Company for its free distribution of medicine in Third World countries to 600,000 victims of River Blindness.

∎ Ben & Jerry's (Vermont ice cream maker), presented to Gail Mayville for designing, lobbying for, and executing environmental programs (e.g., a line that includes nuts from the Brazilian rain forest), which hopes to create a demand for something other than land.

∎ GE Plastics' John Hutt, who started the renovation of nonprofit facilities, such as community school facilities, as corporate "team-building exercises." (382)

Who says business isn't honest? In a study by Arthur D. Little, 85% of executives polled rated price fixing and environmental abuse as serious offenses, 81% rated worker health and safety violations as a serious crime, and 80% rated insider trading as a serious crime. While impressive, one has to wonder about the *other 15–20%* who don't rate these as serious crimes!

Perhaps they only reflect society. The executives appear more concerned about business offenses than the public. While *80%* of corporate executives thought insider trading was an extremely serious offense, only *41%* of the public thought so. While *85%* of executives thought price fixing was extremely serious, only *60%* of the public felt that way. In the area of health and safety violations, 81% of executives felt they were serious crimes while only 74% of the public felt so. (319)

North Carolina National Bank encourages employees to take two hours out of their workweek with pay to volunteer to help area schools. (440, p. 6)

Fallacy: Associations honestly police themselves.

Fact: The American Bar Association estimates that only 0.2% (get real!) of *all* U.S. lawyers are *ever* disciplined by bar committees, and proceedings against the large firms that do major corporate work are virtually unknown. (312) Either lawyers are incredibly honest, or some people are not doing their job!

Fallacy: The most *humane* thing for U.S corporations with operations in South Africa to do was to pull out to protest white supremacist policies there.

Fact: This is a matter of personal judgment. Consider that the 215 American corporations that did pull out took with them their enforcement of fair employment practices and the millions they spent to improve life and working conditions for their employees. For example, Ford Motor Company and other firms paid for housing, schooling, recreation, and health facilities. (58, p. 258)

 IRS dishonest? In a survey by the GAO, questionnaires were mailed to full-time employees of the IRS. In that survey, two-thirds believed the level of integrity in the IRS is generally high or very high. About 10% thought the agency's integrity was low or very low. The surprising fact is that 34% believed at least some upper-level managers engage in misconduct, 40% believed at least some midlevel employees do, and 47% believe at least some staff engage in misconduct. (372, p. 2)

 Invasion of privacy? Kir Plastics, a credit card manufacturer, sends a "special agent" to interview potential employees at their home to evaluate living conditions, observe habits, meet family members, and look for evidence of drug use. (441, p. 4)

Exporting/Importing

Fallacy: We would not have a trade deficit if Japan would open its markets to U.S. goods.

Fact: Some studies show that the U.S. trade deficit would drop only $5–8 billion if Japan did away with all its import barriers. (58, p. 159) The U.S. trade deficit with Japan has run about $50–60 billion a year recently.

Fallacy: The *North American Free Trade Agreements* linking the United States, Canada, and Mexico will simply send more U.S. jobs south to Mexico.

Fact: Only at first. Economists expect that 150,000 more low-skilled manufacturing jobs will go to Mexico during the first three years of the pact. But during that time more jobs will be created for U.S. exporters to handle increased sales to Mexico. Experts predict that the trade pact will produce 135,000 net new U.S. jobs by 1995. Also, the higher wages the pact will bring to Mexico should mean more U.S. exports south of the border and fewer illegal immigrants into the United States for years to come. (139)

Fallacy: The largest importer of vehicles to America is a Japanese company.

Fact: *General Motors and Ford Motor Company* imported more vehicles to America than did any other manufacturer. They were followed by Toyota and Chrysler Corporation, according to figures provided by Toyota. This is because many American-name cars are made somewhere else. For instance, 17% of the Geo Metro Storms are made in Japan, 33% of the Buick Centurys are made in Mexico as are Ford Escorts. Canadians build the Buick Regal and the Ford Crown Victoria. (344, p. 10)

Fallacy: America doesn't focus on exporting as other countries do.

Fact: Over the past 25 years, U.S. exports have grown faster than the economy as a whole. (331) U.S. exports have risen every year since 1985, even while the primary customers for our goods—Canada, Western Europe, and Japan—have suffered economic reverses that crippled their ability to buy our goods. (123)

The international market is more than four times larger than the U.S. market. Growth rates in many overseas markets far outpace domestic market growth. (309)

Fallacy: The United States doesn't need the rest of the world! We are big enough to be self-sufficient.

Fact: That might have been true at one time, but it is not now. If you look at total trade, including exports and imports of goods and services as a share of GNP, then you would find those shares are almost identical for the United States, Japan, and the European Community taken as a group. The United States is as dependent on the world economy as the Japanese. In fact, America's dependence on the world's economy has more than doubled while Japan's and Europe's has stayed about the same. (377, p. 53)

Fallacy: Exporting is widespread among U.S. companies.

Fact: Many U.S. firms of all sizes now export their goods, but only 2,000 companies account for 80% of U.S. exports. (199, p. 72)

Fallacy: Exporting still isn't a very big part of the U.S. economy.

Fact: Exporting has become a *huge* part of the U.S. economy. In 1991, the United States exported $580 billion of goods and services. That was a bigger part of our gross domestic product than auto manufacturing and homebuilding combined. Exports provided most of the economy's growth during 1990 and 1991. And U.S. workers in key exporting industries earn 12% more than those in other industries. (199, p. 68)

———

Fallacy: Japan is the world's largest exporter.

Fact: Guess who is number one (and it is not Japan, they are third), at least as of 1991? *In 1991 the United States recaptured the title as the world's largest exporter.* American businesses sold $422 billion of goods to foreigners, a 7.5% jump from 1990. Germany slipped 4.5% to *second,* and Japan sold $315 billion (but we still have a big trade imbalance with Japan). (245)

18% The United States exports 18% of the world total compared with 13% for West Germany and 12% for Japan. (19, p. 152)

———

Fallacy: Exports are important to the United States.

Fact: They are not simply important, they are *critical.* Consider the facts:

∎ Almost a fifth of U.S. industrial output is exported.

∎ The output from two of every five acres of farmland is exported.

∎ About a third of U.S. corporate profits come from either exports or investments abroad.

∎ Over 5 million American jobs depend on trade. (415)

For every additional billion dollars the United States exports, 25,000 jobs are created. In 1990 alone, the United States exported $30 billion of products to Mexico. (408)

Fallacy: As is true of products, Japan also exports more capital than it imports.

Fact: Usually true, but not in 1991. That year, Japan imported more long-term capital than it exported. That's the first time that has happened since 1980. (271, p. 20)

Fallacy: The Japanese close their markets to American products.

Fact: Since 1985 the United States exports more to Japan than it does to Germany, France, and Italy *combined.* (243)

It is estimated that 30–35% of Japanese exporters share production with developing countries. Less than 5% of U.S. manufacturers do. (93, p. 15)

Fallacy: The United States imports much from other industrialized nations, but not much from developing nations that really need customers.

Fact: In 1987, the United States bought *48%* of all Third World countries' manufactured exports. The European Community, whose GNP is bigger than the United States', took 29% of Third World exports that year, while the Japanese bought 12%. (100, p. 62)

Fallacy: With the increase in sales of goods across borders, industrialized nations are moving toward free and open trade.

Fact: Since 1980, 20 of the 24 largest industrialized nations have tightened restrictions on imports. (42)

━━━

Fallacy: Trade with Japan is very one-sided, with the United States on the short end.

Fact: Japan imports $394 per capita from the United States; the United States imports only $360 per capita from Japan. (243)

━━━

Fallacy: Many Japanese companies export huge amounts of goods to the United States.

Fact: Twenty Japanese firms account for 50% of all exports to the United States; 50 firms account for 75%. (19, p. 167)

━━━

Fallacy: Japan's exports are growing much faster than America's.

Fact: The often-publicized trade data figures may lead you to think this is true. But from 1986 to 1990, the volume of U.S. exports rose 13% a year while Japan's volume only rose 2.8% a year. (60)

━━━

Fallacy: Japanese computer companies are steadily gaining market share in the U.S. personal computer (PC) market.

Fact: *Japanese firms are losing market share* in the U.S. PC market. In laptop and notebook computers, the Japanese share of U.S. unit sales fell from about 39% in 1988 to around 24% in 1992. During the same period, unit sales of Japanese desktop computers hovered around 7%. (152, p. 64)

━━━

 The United States leads the world in revenue from its recorded music. When a song is published or recorded in one country and played in another, the royalties generated are part of the trade accounts. For 1989–1990, the United States held 28% of the world market share of these royalties. Germany was second with 16.1%, followed by France at 11.1%. (169)

∎ Some American products do very well in Japan. Two of the best are Schick razors, which has 69.5% of the Japanese safety razor market, and Coca-Cola, which holds one-third of the soft drink market. (65, p. 82)

The Japanese import more than 60% of the beef and veal Americans sell abroad, more than 30% of their feed grains and corn, and close to 60% of their pork and grapefruit. (19, p. 167)

Fallacy: The voluntary restraints on Japanese subcompact cars imported into the United States during the 1980s *helped* American consumers by holding down prices and by giving U.S. auto companies a chance to match Japanese quality.

Fact: The restrictions hurt consumers. The drop in the supply of Japanese cars let the Japanese raise their prices. Seeing Japanese car prices rise, U.S. car companies also raised their prices. The voluntary quotas cost American consumers about *$1 billion in 1983 alone.* (20, p. 117)

Fallacy: The United States' largest trading partner is Japan.

Fact: No, and it is not Germany either. The United States and Canada trade $200 billion of goods and services annually, more than three times the trade between the United States and Japan. Over 75% of Canadian exports go to the United States. (379)

∎ Canada accounts for over 21% of total U.S. exports and over 18% of total U.S. imports. (Mexico recently replaced Germany as the United States' third largest trading partner). (409)

Japanese factories import three times more, on average, than the typical German- or British-owned plant, and the Japanese rely far less on local suppliers. (339, p. 62)

Fallacy: Japan has some of the world's highest import tariffs.

Fact: Japan's tariffs are among the world's lowest. (20, p. 68)

Fallacy: Japan is the leading exporter of manufactured goods.

Fact: West Germany exported 30% more manufactured goods in 1990 than did either the *United States* or Japan. Industrial cooperatives that help companies solve problems and good research and development are two of the reasons for Germany's exporting success. (53)

Fallacy: The U.S. trade deficit with Japan is *purely* the result of Japanese trade practices.

Fact: There are many reasons for our trade deficit with Japan. One reason of our own making is that our high federal deficit and low savings rate combine to require that we import money to finance our federal deficit. The money we import counts as part of our trade deficit in goods and services. (58, pp. 158–159)

Fallacy: It is only Japan that makes it difficult for American cars to be imported into their country.

Fact: Consider how tough it is to crack the Chinese auto market. We must give two free samples, pay about $40,000 for testing the cars, and pay for Chinese officials to travel to the plant where the cars were built to inspect the plant. (58, p. 176)

Fallacy: Our trade deficit is primarily due to Japanese automakers.

Fact: *Imported oil is a major cause.* The United States imported more oil in 1989 than in any year since 1979, accounting for 46% of the nation's demand. That cost some $49 billion, which accounted for 44% of the U.S. trade deficit. (387)

The United States imports 290 billion barrels of oil each year from Iraq and Kuwait combined. If we could raise the fuel efficiency of U.S. autos by 2.75 miles per gallon, the United States could save 290 billion barrels of oil per year. (88)

 The U.S. government allows two peanuts per capita to be imported into the country each year. (90) (Isn't that about the same as the number of autos per capita the government allows to be imported?)

Fallacy: Europe's markets are opening as the European Community becomes a reality.

Fact: European markets are becoming more protectionist in some ways, one of which is the granting of state subsidies to their companies. These averaged $115 billion a year during the 1980s, and there is no slowdown in sight. (58, p. 122)

Fallacy: Only large companies export.

Fact: According to the U.S. Small Business Administration, of the approximately 90,000 firms that had export sales in 1988, 25% were firms with fewer than 100 employees. (228)

■ Cal Pacific exports disposable wooden chopsticks to—you've got it—Japan! Since the Japanese do not have a readily available supply of lumber, they import some 130,000,000 chopsticks every single day. (228)

■ Win some, lose some. Americans imported 300,000 American flags made in Taiwan during the first four months of 1990. (22, p. 62)

∎ Computers are America's most exported item. (224)

Fallacy: Foreign aid from developed nations to Third World nations is the only feasible way to provide money for development and for solving environmental problems in Third World nations.

Fact: The World Bank estimates that if the United States, Japan, and the European Community would lower their trade barriers by 50%, it would increase exports from developing countries by $50 billion a year. That is about the amount of foreign aid that went to developing countries in 1991. (101)

Financial

 Forty-seven of the 50 largest banks in the world are *not* American, and the 6 largest are Japanese. (261, p. 2)

Fallacy: We don't need foreign money.

Fact: There was a 10% chance that a dollar loaned to a U.S. business in 1992 came from *a Japanese bank.* (42)

Fallacy: American managers tend to have a short-term perspective.

Fact: Short-term thinking by managers is the symptom, not the cause. A poll taken in September 1987 asked 400 chief executive officers which agents were putting the most pressure on them for short-term performance. Fifty-eight percent of the CEOs said that *institutional owners* (e.g., pension funds and insurance companies) are a principal source of pressure. What's more, a 1985 survey of large institutional owners showed that only 4% considered the quality of a company's products (normally an important factor in long-term competitiveness) in selecting stocks for their portfolio. (322)

Institutional ownership in the market is increasing and chief executive officers know it. Ninety-eight percent of these CEOs said they had kept or gained influence, and it's true. In 1949, institutions owned 12% of shares listed on the New York Stock Exchange. It had grown to 16% by 1976 and to almost 50% by 1984. Institutional ownership in the chemical industry went from 15% in 1976 to 52% in 1984. (322)

By 1984, institutional investors held about 60% of shares of U.S. corporations. Most of the institutional ownership has been fueled by growth in pension funds following the passage of the Employee Retirement Income Security Act of 1974. By the year 2000, pension funds are expected to hold 50% of all corporate equity in the United States. (322)

Institutional investment is much more concentrated in Japan than in the United States. Compare the number of firms in each country:

Type of Company	United States	Japan
Commercial banks	14,000+	158
Life insurance companies	1,500	24
Property-casualty insurers	1,800	23

Source: Ref. 116, p. 156

Fallacy: Japan's large banks do not make bad loans as some of America's large banks made during the 1980s.

Fact: In 1992, Japanese banks held $215 billion in bad debts, amounting to 5% of all their loans. Japan's top 21 banks carried two-thirds of these bad loans. The worst loans were those made to property developers. About 70% of these borrowers were not even paying the interest on their loans. (64, p. 56)

Fallacy: Toyota is concerned with market share, not cash flow.

 Fact: In 1990, Toyota had enough cash to buy both Ford and Chrysler at current stock prices and have $5 billion left. (36, p. 69)

Fallacy: The richest company in the world is an American oil or auto company.

Fact: Toyota Motor Company is the wealthiest company in the world, with $13.7 billion (in 1990) in cash and marketable securities. Ford, not General Motors, is the richest American corporation, with $6.5 billion in cash and marketable securities. Of the 26 wealthiest international corporations, 19 are Japanese, and 3 are American (Ford, Boeing, and IBM). (335, p. 94)

∎ In 1980, foreign investors owned $268 billion of the United States' primary debt securities and $106 billion of the common stock outstanding. By the end of 1988, those commitments had risen dramatically to $586 billion for debt and $193 billion for common stock. Foreign investors held $1.2 trillion of U.S. financial assets in 1988. In other words *we are the world's largest debtor nation.* (328)

 Long-term and short-term corporate debt outstanding in the United States doubled from 1980 to 1988. (328)

Living beyond our means? Total private and public debt outstanding was $4.05 trillion at the end of 1980, rising to $9.51 trillion at the end of 1988. That is an annual growth rate of 11%. Over the same period, our gross national product (GNP) increased from $2.58 trillion to $4.86 trillion, an annual growth rate of 8%. The growth in our debt outstripped the growth of our GNP. (328)

———

Fallacy: Knowing a process has a high return on investment for a business means it will be implemented.

Fact: The Department of Defense has saved billions through value engineering (VE), a procedure for challenging both an activity and how it is done. The Environmental Protection Agency estimates a rate of return of 20:1 for every dollar invested in the VE process. Despite its potential, the U.S. Postal Service has no goals, not a single employee assigned full time to VE or trained in the technique in the past five years, or, as of 1987, any record of receiving any VE proposal during that time. (308)

———

Fallacy: Company size is the safest way to get job security.

Fact: Over *40%* of the *Fortune* 500 companies that existed between 1975 and 1985 no longer exist. (318)

———

Fallacy: The Japanese are buying everything in the United States!

Fact: Japanese investment in U.S. firms is much in the news. But by 1990, *British* holdings in the United States were much larger than Japanese holdings. In the first half of that year, the British bought $7.9 billion of American assets, the French $5.7 billion, and, in third place, the Japanese bought only $3.8 billion. It is important also to note that U.S. holdings abroad still exceeded foreign holdings here. (20, p. 137)

———

Fallacy: The Japanese are out to take all they can from us.

Fact: Maybe so, but they are doing their fair share of giving, too. By 1994, CEOs of Japanese firms plan to give about $1 billion to American charities, about 8% of all corporate donations. (20, p. 143)

Fallacy: Foreign-owned firms in the United States pay their American workers less than American-owned firms pay theirs.

Fact: The opposite is true. In 1986, the average employee of a foreign-owned manufacturing firm earned $32,887. The figure for American-owned firms was $28,945. (20, p. 147)

———

Fallacy: The annual returns on common stocks and long-term bonds are greatly affected by the rate of inflation.

Fact: Although many believe this to be true, it is not. A study by Ibbotson Associates found almost no relationship between the rate of inflation and historical annual returns on common stocks or long-term corporate or government bonds during the years 1929–1990. (447)

———

Fallacy: Market timing—investing one's money in the stock market only during the days when the market rises the most—*is not* a risky investment strategy.

Fact: Market timing *is* a risky strategy and can cost an investor substantial returns. Assume that you were an investor during the 2,528 trading days from 1980 to 1989 and that whenever your money was not invested in stocks it was earning interest at the average rate for 30-day Treasury bills. Further assume that when your money *was* in stocks it was earning the same rate as the often-quoted Standard & Poor's 500 index for that period. Under these assumptions, if your money was in stocks all but the 10 days when the stock market rose the most, your money would have earned 12.6%. But if you had kept your money in stocks for the full 2,528 days, you would have earned a 17.5% return. The message: Market timing is a risky strategy; get in the market and stay. (448, p. 6)

———

Fallacy: Homeowners are the chief beneficiaries of the wave of home refinancing in 1992.

Fact: Would you believe refinancing might be your patriotic duty? Homeowners benefited by saving thousands of dollars in interest on their home mortgages. But over 40% of them refi-nanced from a 30-year to a 15-year loan. This could mean that the U.S. Treasury becomes the chief beneficiary because tax collections will rise. One estimate has it that at 1992 interest and marginal tax rates, each dollar of shortened debt cuts the present value of the government's home buyers' subsidy by $7,000 for each $100,000 financed. Based on estimated 1992 home refinancing, this could mean about $13 billion more (in 1992 dollars) in tax collections over the next 30 years. So refinancing your house can be a very patriotic action! (98)

∎ The Resolution Trust Corporation (RTC), formed to sell the assets of failed savings and loan associations, must pay maintenance, taxes, and insurance on the buildings and land it holds until a buyer is found. These expenses can amount to 20% of the book value of an empty office building over a one-year period. Since 1989, the RTC has paid $1 million for the upkeep of its largest asset, the 23,250-acre Banning-Lewis ranch near Colorado Springs, Colorado. If you would like to own this little spread with its view of the Rocky Mountains, the RTC would be happy—*very* happy—to sell it to you for a mere $24 million! (454, pp. 117–118)

Foreign Competition

Fallacy: As a manufacturer, your primary competition is probably a company in the United States.

Fact: Used to be that way, but not any more! In 1985, only 5% of U.S. manufacturers in an A. T. Kearney survey placed a foreign company among their top five competitors. By 1990, 30% reported that *two of their top five* competitors were foreign; almost 45% projected three or more of their top five competitors would be foreign by 1992. (332, p. 50)

———

Fallacy: Your business has no foreign competitor.

Fact: The Commerce Department estimated that in 1984, in U.S. domestic markets, some 70% of U.S. firms faced "significant foreign competition." By 1987, the chairman of the Foreign Trade Council estimated the figure to be 80%. (325, p. 11)

———

Over 70% of U.S. industries surveyed indicated that they were under full-scale attack by foreign competitors. (252)

———

Fallacy: We in the United States are the ones *most* in favor of "free trade."

Fact: In a study by *Harvard Business Review,* when the question was asked, 95% of Germans, 86% of Japanese, 83% of Brazilians, 79% of French, and only 78% of Americans favored free trade. (13, p. 156)

———

Fallacy: The world thinks of the United States as leading the fight for free trade.

Fact: The Organization for Economic Cooperation and Development recently surveyed its members, the 24 richest countries in the world. It found that only four had reduced their barriers to trade over the last decade: Australia, New Zealand, Turkey, and Japan! It happens that those 4 were the most protective at the start of the period. The other 20 countries, including the United States, erected *new* trade barriers, quotas, voluntary restraints, and so on over the last decade. (377, p. 62)

———

Fallacy: As airlines are deregulated in Europe during the 1990s, consumers there should see fare reductions proportional to those in the United States during the deregulated 1980s.

Fact: Not likely, for three reasons:

1. European Economic Community (EC) countries will have the right to object to fare cuts they think are below competitive levels.

2. Low-cost charter outfits carry most of the bargain-hunting vacation flyers in Europe. The business flyers who remain demand a certain level of service, for which they are willing to pay.

3. European flights are shorter, and there are numerous modern superhighways. Only 2% of travelers fly between major European cities, compared to 14% in the United States. (458, pp. 88–89)

———

 **Fallacy:** The U.S. market is open to competition from foreign airlines.

Fact: Not always. While United Airlines and Delta Air Lines are building hubs in Europe, the United States bars European airlines from transporting passengers within the United States. (48, p. 55)

Fallacy: One field in which the United States dominates the world market is in commercial aircraft.

Fact: As recently as 1987, Boeing and McDonnell Douglas delivered more than 90% of jet aircraft. But by 1992 Airbus Industrie of Europe sold 30% of all new aircraft and is gaining market share. Airbus has sold to 14 of the world's 17 largest airlines. Airbus is attacking the only U.S. product whose sales abroad have achieved a positive trade balance every year since World War II. (66, pp. 102–103)

Fallacy: When an airline buys planes from Europe instead of the United States, *all* production jobs associated with producing the planes are lost to Europeans.

Fact: Not so. For example, parts representing 20–30% of each European-made Airbus plane are made by American workers from nearly 59 companies located in 34 states. (66, p. 108)

By the way, the reverse also is true. Japanese companies produce many of the parts of a Boeing aircraft. As is the case for autos, the commercial aircraft industry is a global one.

 In 1980, American producers accounted for 53% of global sales of semiconductors, 75% of semiconductor equipment revenues, and 70% of computer sales. Those shares later fell to 44%, 47%, and 67%, respectively. (339, p. 62)

■ Talk about foreign competition; it can be brutal! How much ground have U.S. companies lost to the Japanese in making the basic components that will lead to success in the global computer industry? All major producers of materials and equipment for making semiconductors were American in 1980. By 1990, four of the top five companies were Japanese. (15, p. 68)

Fallacy: Japanese semiconductor equipment companies lead their U.S. rivals in revenue and world market share.

Fact: The preceding fact might lead you to think so. But in 1992, U.S. semiconductor equipment companies increased their revenues 17% to $5.5 billion, ringing up a 53% world market share. By contrast, their Japanese rivals saw revenues drop 13% to $3.9 billion, which amounted to 38% of the world market. (168)

Fallacy: The U.S. computer industry's world market share only fell from 70% in 1980 to 60% in 1990. Japan held only a 20% share in 1990. This shows that the U.S. computer industry is pretty secure.

Fact: The U.S. position is very insecure. You must remember that market share is measured in gross revenue. Some of that revenue must be paid to suppliers. U.S. and European computer companies are paying more and more of their revenue to Japanese selling to suppliers of hardware and components. One forecast sees the Japanese supplying over 50% of worldwide hardware content by 1995. (107, pp. 55–56)

Fallacy: The United States has lost its global lead only in a few technologies.

Fact: If only it were true! But the U.S. Council on Competitiveness recently found that we still lead only in about one-third of the technologies critical to the global economy in the next century. According to this report, we have fallen behind in another third and are struggling to stay competitive with other countries in the final third of important technologies. It looks as if we have our work cut out for us! (84, p. 79)

 What threat? In 1991, 22% of Japanese said that the Soviet Union was the greatest threat to Japan, and 24% said the United States was the greatest threat! Perhaps the Japanese are not overly concerned about any threat because only 10% were willing to fight for their country. (85)

Fallacy: When it comes to being the world economic leader, the United States' main competitive threat comes from the East, notably Japan.

Fact: John Hillkirk, a *USA Today* writer, attended the Business Education Forum in Tucson, Arizona, in 1990. He asked 25 CEOs and university presidents in attendance which nation or nations would lead the world economically at the turn of the century if our competitive position does not improve significantly. Five said the United States, 6 said Japan, 4 said Europe and Japan, but almost half (10) said the *unified European Community,* and none said a reunified Germany. Stay tuned! (390)

Fallacy: The Japanese will take the lead in high-definition television (HDTV) as they have with other consumer electronic products.

Fact: The HDTV products American firms are bringing to market represent a higher-resolution version of the technology than do the HDTV products from Japan. Japanese HDTV technology has little chance of being adopted in America or in Europe. (57, p. A10)

The Russians are coming, the Russians are coming! No, make that the Japanese. A recent count showed 200,000 Japanese residing in the United States, with more coming. (16, p. 115) Over 400,000 people work for Japanese companies in the United States. About 35,000 Americans take college courses in Japanese, and enrollment is rising. More than 1 million Americans visited Japan in 1990. This is 40% more than five years ago. Three million Japanese visited the United States, most as tourists or students. (16, p. 118)

Every state except North Dakota is home to at least one Japanese-affiliated factory, most of them wholly owned by a Japanese company. As of September 1991, Japanese companies owned 10% or more of 1,563 plants employing about 350,000. (271, p. 16)

Fallacy: The Japanese may be invading the United States with their products, but at least they never invaded the continental U.S. *militarily.*

Fact: Oh, but one of them did. Japanese Chief Flying Officer Nobuo Fujita was launched from a submarine in a single-engine float plane on September 9, 1942. His aircraft carried two 170-pound incendiary bombs that he dropped in the Oregon forest. He intended for these bombs to start tremendous fires that would strike fear in Americans' hearts. Fortunately for us, the forests were so wet that the bombs did little damage. A second attack by Fujita three weeks later outside Port Oxford also failed to do much damage.

Fujita's specific purpose was to retaliate for Colonel Jimmy Doolittle's air raids on Tokyo. He visited Oregon one more time—20 years later, at the request of the Brookings, Oregon, Junior Chamber of Commerce. (163)

Fallacy: American industry is not competitive!

Fact: As of the early 1990s, the average American auto had 1.5 defects, according to J. D. Power and Associates. This is down from 7 defects in 1981. That's closing in on the 1.1 defect rate for Japanese cars. Ford Motor Company's 1991 cars averaged fewer defects than Nissans, Mazdas, and Mitsubishis. (207, p. 70)

Fallacy: In the aftermath of World War II, the Japanese freely chose the automobile industry as a major target for expansion.

Fact: Events for which the United States is responsible had much to do with launching the post–World War II growth of the Japanese auto industry. U.S. forces destroyed Japan's aircraft industry during the war. This directed many of Japan's best engineers to the auto industry instead of the aircraft industry, where they normally go. Also, the American authorities would not allow aeronautical engineering departments in Japanese universities in postwar Japan. This policy also drove engineers into Japan's auto industry. (112, p. 283)

———

Fallacy: America's falling share of the global economy—from 50% in 1950 to 25% in 1990—shows that our nation truly is in economic decline.

Fact: Not if one looks at the history of this century. America's huge share of the global economy in the post–World War II years shows how little competition we faced from other industrialized nations that were devastated by the war. It was inevitable that these nations would rebuild their shattered economies, especially with the United States helping them to do so. It should be of little surprise, then, that America's current 25% of the global economy matches its pre–World War II share. Despite the decline in global share, the U.S. gross national product is twice that of Japan, three times larger than the former Soviet Union's, and four times that of Germany. (58, pp. 25–26)

———

Fallacy: The problem of "dumping" (selling a product in a foreign market at its cost of production) is a recent phenomenon.

Fact: Early in the twentieth century, the United States and Canada enacted laws to deal with this practice. During and after World War I, the U.S. Congress adopted several antidumping statutes. The first was in 1916. (370, p. 8)

———

Fallacy: Japanese high-tech companies work alone; they do not like to share their technology with foreign companies.

Fact: This past practice is changing. Consider Sony's recent extensive joint ventures with Apple Computer in notebook computer and personal digital electronic products. Also, for years, Toshiba has shared semiconductor technology with Motorola. More recently, Toshiba began a joint venture with IBM to build flat-panel displays. Toshiba also has partnerships with General Electric, Time Warner, and German Electric giant Siemens. (62)

Fallacy: Japan's Ministry of International Trade and Industry (MITI) almost dictates the markets in which major Japanese corporations will compete.

Fact: Not so. The Ministry considers the competitive and economic impact a new market might have on Japan and advises industry leaders accordingly. But the development of Japan's auto industry shows that MITI *does not* dictate to industry leaders. Around 1960, MITI opposed expansion of the industry because it required petroleum and iron ore—two raw materials in very short supply in Japan. (111)

Fallacy: Only recently has there been a movement for a unified Europe.

Fact: At a peace conference in Paris on August 21, *1849,* writer-statesman Victor Hugo called for the establishment of a United States of Europe. (44, p. 46)

 When Western Europe becomes unified, and when capital goods and services freely cross borders, it will mean

▪ A $260 billion increase in goods and services.

▪ An additional 1.8 million new jobs.

▪ A combined GNP of $5 trillion.

▪ A population of 355 million (compared to the U.S. population of 250 million). (302)

 The reunified Germany has an economy larger than that of *all* the Eastern European countries *combined,* including the countries of the old Soviet Union. (302)

Fallacy: The new European Community everyone is talking about will be the world's largest free market.

Fact: It will be big but not as large as the U.S. trading zone when we add Mexico and Canada to the present free trade zone with the United States. Doing that would yield the world's biggest free market. It would have 364 million consumers. Total output would be $6 trillion per year, which is 25% more than the ECs. (11, p. 32)

———

Fallacy: Americans strongly believe government should actively help domestic business compete internationally.

Fact: Our citizens were less supportive of that idea than the citizens of other major industrialized countries. (13, pp. 158–159)

———

Fallacy: European auto companies will *really* dominate the European auto market as the European Community becomes stronger.

Fact: Not according to estimates, one of which forecasts that the Japanese may capture 19.5% and Americans 25.5% of the European auto market by the year 2000. In 1990, the Japanese had 12.6% and Americans had 22.8% of that market. (43, p. 149)

———

Fallacy: The economic wall of the coming European Community will effectively block Japanese competition.

Fact: Douglas McWilliams, chief economist at the Confederation of British Industry, predicts that by the year 2000, 16% of British factory workers will have Japanese bosses. Germans buy 40% of Japanese exports to Europe. There are already cracks in the wall. EC headquarters in Brussels wants a six-year transition to a free market. France wants British-built Japanese cars counted as Japanese rather than as European.

Britain, Germany, and Japan are all fighting the French plan. It seems unlikely that Europe will erect a solid wall against Japan. (10, pp. 48–49) Japanese competition in Europe is now serious in autos, computers, consumer electronics, tires, and semiconductors. It is moderate in cellular communications and printers. (10, pp. 46–47)

Fallacy: The United Europe really is united.

Fact: Not by a long shot. For example, the German leadership favors a Common European Currency. But the most recent polls available in the spring of 1992 showed that 72% of Germans oppose trading the Deutsche mark for this currency. (74)

———

Fallacy: We are becoming less and less dependent on foreign oil.

Fact: The Congressional Office of Technology Assessment projects that by 2010 the United States may still depend on imports for nearly 70% of total supply (an amount one consultant estimates it would take 36 supertankers a day to deliver). (246)

———

Fallacy: The United States has enough oil of its own.

Fact: We are running out of recoverable oil. Known reserves that can be extracted at current market prices have been declining almost steadily for 22 years, and the current supplies of 26 billion barrels would last the nation *barely four years* at present usage rates. (246)

———

McDonald's of Japan knows how to be competitive in foreign countries. Den Fujita says exporters should study cultural aspects very carefully. Unlike their approach in the United States, McDonald's in Japan avoided U.S.-style suburban sites and, instead, focused on urban shopping centers where people tend to congregate. It targeted all advertising at younger people because the habits of older Japanese are very difficult to change. It even changed the pronunciation of its name to

"Macudonaldo" because it found Japanese had difficulty pronouncing its name. (320)

━━━━━━

 Foreign pronunciation was also a problem for Coca-Cola in China. When it entered the Chinese market in 1982, its translation in Chinese meant "bite the wax tadpole." After some consultation, the Chinese characters now used mean "permit the mouth to rejoice." (320)

━━━━━━

Fallacy: Japan (or Germany or Taiwan) is the most economically dynamic country on the planet.

Fact: It is a loaded question! Whichever of the three you choose, you would be wrong! It is tiny *Singapore,* if you measure economic growth mile for mile. Only one-fifth the size of Rhode Island, Singapore has few resources other than the will of its people by which to achieve its 7% annual growth rate. (58, p. 239)

━━━━━━

Fallacy: Singapore's booming economy stems from its power as a banking center.

Fact: Banking is only part of Singapore's strength now. More than 650 multinational corporations have manufacturing operations there. Over 60% of all computer disk drives are made there. Singapore boasts the world's largest VCR factory and largest compressor factory. Apple Computer finds it to be 40–50% cheaper to automate manufacturing there than in the United States. Do you begin to see why Singapore is one of the so-called "little tiger" nations?

Maybe we could take a lesson from Singapore about government operations as well as business operations. Each year the Singapore government tries to recruit the top 3% of the nation's college graduates for civil service. Pay raises for all government employees are based on how well the economy performs! How's that for a novel idea?

Bear in mind that government vision and planning do play a key role in the performance of the Singaporean economy. Here are some of the impressive achievements of this public-private partnership in the country that some are beginning to call a nation-corporation:

∎ World's best telecommunications infrastructure (the United States ranks second, Japan third)

∎ Most pagers per citizen

∎ Work force rated world's best in each of the past 10 years.

∎ World's highest savings rate (45%)

∎ World's busiest and most efficient port (83, pp. 42, 45)

Fallacy: The failure rates for the inability of managers to adjust to foreign culture are the same for Europeans, Japanese, and Americans.

Fact: American failure rates are much higher. One-half of U.S. companies had failure rates of 10–20%, and 7% of U.S. companies had failure rates of 30%. Meanwhile, a majority of West European firms had recall rates under 5%. About one-third had recall rates of 6–10%, and only 3% had failure rates of 11–15%. The vast majority of Japanese firms had failure rates below 5%, while only a scant 10% of those firms had recall rates of 6–10%, and 14% of the Japanese firms had 11–19%. (310)

Foreign Investment

 Who's buying whom? During the 10-year period ending in 1988, America increased its investment overseas by about 180%. Foreigners, during that same period, increased their investment in the United States by about 380%. At the end of 1988, foreign investment in the United States totaled $1,786 billion with about *$329 billion* in direct investment. The rest was in U.S. corporate bonds, government securities, and claims on U.S. banks. Meanwhile, the U.S. investment totaled $1,254 billion with its direct investment overseas at a comparable *$327 billion.* Thus the United States has about the same direct investment abroad as there is foreign direct investment in the United States. (337)

Fallacy: Japanese investment in the United States is increasing dramatically (translation "They are buying *everything!*").

Fact: It's down, way down. The U.S. Department of Commerce estimates net investment in all U.S. businesses by Japan fell precipitously to $4.3 billion in 1991 compared to $17 billion during each of the three previous years. (271, p. 20)

 The National Association of Realtors estimated that in 1986 the total value of all foreign real estate holdings was only about 1.5% of nonfarm, nonresidential real estate assets in the United States. So what about farm or agricultural acreage? In 1988, foreign persons held only 1% of U.S. agricultural acreage. The biggest investor in this acreage was the United Kingdom, followed by Canada, France, and Germany. (433)

—————

Fallacy: The Japanese are the largest foreign investors in U.S. Treasury notes. Should they drastically lower these investments while the U.S. federal deficit is still high, U.S. interest rates would rise dramatically.

Fact: The Japanese bought about half of U.S. Treasury notes during the late 1980s. By 1992, they were net sellers. Several foreign countries invest in U.S. Treasury notes, but the biggest buyer in 1992 was Taiwan, partly because it became the world's largest holder of foreign currency reserves (over $80 billion). Much of these reserves are in dollars that the country must constantly reinvest. Thanks to cash-rich Taiwan and Singapore, another big buyer of U.S. Treasury notes, the feared rise in U.S. interest rates did not occur when Japan left the market. (127, p. C1)

—————

Fallacy: Japan is the primary country investing in America.

Fact: Foreign direct investment comes largely from three geographic areas: (1) the United Kingdom, with $102 billion; (2) Japan, with $53 billion; and surprisingly close behind (3) the Netherlands, with $49 billion. On the U.S. side, three-fourths of its direct investment is in developed countries, namely, (1) Canada at $61 billion, (2) Great Britain at $48 billion, and (3) West Germany at $22 billion. Investment by the United States in Japan (as of 1989) was only $17 billion. (337)

—————

In the early 1960s, long before Sony Corporation ever invested in the United States, it needed capital for expansion. To get it, Sony became the first Japanese company to be listed on the New York Stock Exchange and thus to sell part of its equity to American investors. (84, p. 81)

—————

∎ So you think it is hard to decide how to invest your money? Consider the Japanese investing chore. Japan's private sector and corporate sector generate over $1 billion of surplus capital *every day* that must be invested somewhere. That is $1,000 million every day. Life is tough, isn't it? (19, pp. 159–160)

─────

Four-fifths of Japanese investment in Europe is in services, particularly finance and insurance. (396, p. 10)

─────

Fallacy: Foreigners buying up American commercial properties is bad for America.

Fact: According to the U.S. General Accounting Office, industry experts generally consider foreign investments, in the aggregate, to be beneficial. They are a source of stable long-term capital that does not threaten national security. (368, pp. 2–3)

Industry analysts and academic experts also believe that overall, foreign investment in U.S. real estate is beneficial. They say not only does it constitute a source of stable, long-term capital, but it is also beneficial because it cannot be quickly disposed of or removed from the country. There are no national security concerns or transfers of high technology. Analysts also state that the U.S. real estate market is generally too large and broad to be overwhelmed by outside control. The inflow of foreign capital helped enhance the value of U.S. commercial property markets by providing liquidity. (368, p. 4)

─────

Fallacy: Foreign investment in U.S. assets is bad for America.

Fact: Between 1987 and 1990, the Big Three American auto companies laid off 9,063 American auto workers while the Japanese hired 11,050. In 1992, Japanese-owned automakers plan to make or buy within the United States at least 75% of the content of their American cars. That is a higher percentage than American-owned automakers can boast. (20, p. 128) In 1990, over *one-fourth of U.S. exports bore the label of Japanese-owned companies* (for example, Honda Accords built in Ohio and exported to Japan). Japanese-owned companies accounted for 10% of U.S. exports. These are important facts to consider when judging whether or not foreign investment in the United States is good or bad. (20, p. 129)

———

Fallacy: The United States doesn't need foreign investment.

Fact: *One-fourth* of U.S. business loans come from foreign sources. (415)

———

Fallacy: Whenever foreigners invest in the United States, they almost always make a financial killing.

Fact: The ballyhoo about the Japanese buying Rockefeller Center, the famed Pebble Beach Golf course, and Columbia Pictures tends to reinforce this view. But many agree that the Japanese paid far too much for these and other assets that were past their prime. For example, the Japanese investor who purchased the Pebble Beach Golf course for $800 million in 1990 sold it in 1992 for less than $600 million.

It is nothing new to see foreigners buying at the top of the market. Foreigners were heavy buyers in the U.S. stock market in 1929 and 1969, just as these great bull markets were ending. Foreigners continued to invest in the canal building boom in the United States right up to the collapse of bonds and stocks in 1842, although American investors realized in 1837 that the real growth in that market was over. (61)

———

 It takes two to tango. One study shows that joint ventures between firms based in different countries that have a 50–50 ownership split between the partners have a *60% success rate.* Similar joint ventures in which one partner holds a majority ownership stake have only a *31%* success rate. (73, p. 132)

———

 All foreign affiliates owned around only 2% of the value of total U.S. commercial property in 1988 (latest data available). Foreign direct investment capital in the U.S. commercial *real estate* sector increased fourfold over nine years to $35.85 billion in 1989, with a major share of the increase coming from Japanese investors. Foreign investors have focused on high-profile, high-value, "investment-grade" office buildings and hotels, generally in downtown locations in major cities. Even so, total foreign direct investment in real estate maintained a constant share of 9–10% of total foreign direct investment in all sectors during the 1980s. Japan, the United Kingdom, Canada, the Netherlands, and the Netherlands Antilles together accounted for 83.9% of total foreign investment in the United States. (368, pp. 2–3)

Fallacy: Japanese firms have almost endless access to cheap money.

Fact: This seemed to be true until the Japanese economic recession of 1991–1992. With the Nikkei stock average plunging, their foreign real estate investments going sour, and Japanese investors demanding cash, the cost of money in Japan has risen. For example, several major Japanese firms soon will have to repay the bonds that investors gladly bought during better times because the bonds were convertible into stock. But now investors want cash rather than stock because stock prices have fallen so much. To pay off these bonds in cash, the Japanese will have to borrow at 6%. (63, p. 52) The cost of capital in Japan is becoming about the same as it is in the rest of the world. As a result, soon we may be able to dispel one more fallacy.

Fallacy: Japanese chief executives are much more concerned about gaining market share than they are about profits.

Fact: Because of Japan's rising cost of capital, it follows logically that CEOs there must develop a newfound interest in profits.

Japanese CEOs also must become interested in profits to keep their investors happy. Why is this needed now and not before? Because of the recession of 1991–1992. If investors begin selling their shares of Japanese companies, the cross-holdings of corporate allies such as suppliers and banks will weaken the famed *kieretsu* system and make some firms vulnerable to takeovers. (63, p. 53) Some CEOs will seek to raise profits as a defense against takeovers.

∎ Buy American! Foreign investment in U.S. securities, bonds, factories, and real estate jumped from $235 billion in 1980 to $986 billion in 1990. The federal government owed foreigners $38 billion in 1991 for interest on their investment in debt instruments in this country. This is almost 20% of what U.S. manufacturers expected to invest in capital goods and facilities that year. (17, pp. 17–18)

Fallacy: Americans are very upset about foreign ownership of their resources.

Fact: The rest of the industrialized world is more worried about foreign ownership of U.S. resources than Americans are. (13, pp. 158–159)

 Why are foreigners interested in U.S real estate? A much higher proportion of properties in the United States is controlled by individuals and families than by institutions. As a result, U.S. property changes ownership more often than does property in other countries. In Japan, most investment-grade buildings are owned by large institutions that rarely sell real estate (such sales might be seen as a sign of institutional weakness). U.S. yields on commercial property have been in the 8–10% range compared to 1–2% in Japan and 4–6% in Europe. Recently, though, the yield in Europe has gone to 7–8% while the yield in the United States fell to around 6–8%. (368, p. 10)

Foreign Investment by America

Americans spent $15 billion in 1989 buying companies in Europe; that's *nine times* as much as the Japanese spent for that purpose. (383, p. 14)

Times are a changin'. In 1950, one-half of American investment was in developing countries, compared with only one-sixth today. Almost one-half of American investment is in Europe. WOW! (396, p. 6)

Fallacy: American-owned companies mainly invest overseas so they can economically sell their products back home.

Fact: American-owned companies sell $525 billion of goods and services from European subsidiaries each year, or *six times* as much as American firms back home export to Europe. Of this $525 billion, only 5% is sold back to the American firms' customers in the United States. The other 95% is sold locally or regionally. The same pattern exists for investment in Southeast Asia. American firms' sales back to their American customers account for only one-third of their total sales. Conclusion: Companies should not build overseas because it is the best place to serve a global market, but should invest

115

because it is the *best place to serve a local market* (e.g., Europe or Southeast Asia). (396, p. 7)

Incidentally, foreign firms locating in America do not choose to locate here because of the American technology or work force. They only export an average of 7% of what they sell; thus 93% is sold to Americans. (396, p. 7)

Future Facts and Fallacies

 In 1960 AT&T predicted 3 million picturephones would be in the United States by the late 1980s. (298)

General Electric predicted laser devices will vaporize household garbage; Philco foresees an air filter installed just inside the front door of every home to remove dust and lint from clothing. (298)

 It was also predicted in the 1960s that there would be lawn-cutting robots (programmable for hand-to-hand combat in wartime), as well as infrared night vision for cars, automated bed-making machines, and a tooth decay vaccine. All these predictions were made, according to Steven P. Schnaars of Baruch College, New York, who researched them. (298)

Here are some interesting missed estimates:

■ At the beginning of the twentieth century, some scientists thought the supply of wood was almost gone, and they saw no substitute.

117

■ The radio was initially viewed as a backup when the telegraph lines went down.

■ In 1956, IBM executives said they were not interested in building computers because there would be a market for only about 10 big ones.

■ In 1963, a reputable academician estimated the "automation crisis" would eliminate 1 million jobs per year, wiping out almost *all* jobs by 1999. (39, p. 3)

Health Care

Fact: Today, $1 of every $9 spent in the United States goes to health care. (430)

 How expensive, available, and efficient is health care in America? Consider the following facts.

■ The United States is the only developed nation that leaves 15% of its people *uninsured.*

■ Medical costs are rising more than *twice* as fast as the rate of inflation. Health care consumes *50%* more of national output than it does for any of our closest rivals. If trends continue, it will consume 17% of gross national product (GNP) by the year 2000. *That is more than education, defense, and recreation combined* now absorb. (27, p. 44)

■ Many people's health starts to deteriorate rapidly after age 75. The United States now has 13.2 million people of that age, up from 5.6 million 30 years ago. We may have 21 million of them by the year 2020. (27, p. 45)

■ Robert Brook of the Rand Corporation estimates that up to *one-third* of what Americans spend on medical care is *unnecessary.* Eliminating a small part of this waste would save over $15 billion, the amount needed to give the uninsured coverage. (27, p. 46)

■ Hospital overbuilding during the 1970s followed by Medicare pressure to discharge patients quickly in the 1980s caused the

U.S. hospital bed occupancy rate to drop to 65%. This compares to an 87% rate in Germany and an 81% rate in Canada. As a result, hospitals try to attract doctors who will bring in patients likely to run up big bills. (27, p. 46) Expensive hospitals survive because many companies allow employees to get treatment almost anywhere they like. (27, p. 46)

Fallacy: Health care costs are leveling off.

Fact: U.S. health care spending between 1960 and 1992 increased from 6% to about 14% of gross domestic product. A Health Care Financing Administration estimate indicates that 43.7% of the GDP could be absorbed by health care expenditures by the year 2030. (431, p. 25)

Fallacy: Compared to other developed countries, the United States has an adequate number of doctors.

Fact: This is a widely believed fallacy, but the facts refute it. In 1992, the United States had 2.3 doctors for every 1,000 people, compared to 2.9 in Germany and 2.6 in France. The shortage of U.S. doctors becomes more visible when you consider that 87% of U.S. hospitals are trying to hire doctors. In 1991, 86% of doctors finishing their residency got at least 50 job inquiries. Over 100 U.S. counties have no doctor. Between 1987 and 1992, over 200 rural hospitals closed, many because they had no physicians. (451, pp. 104, 106)

The U.S. General Accounting Office reports that "14% to 32% of surgical procedures, and 7% to 19% of hospital admissions are inappropriate." (422, pp. 1849)

Three of every five visits to a physician result in the doctor prescribing a medication for the patient. (452)

Fallacy: American affluence, health care, and high living standards give its citizens one of the lowest infant mortality rates in the world.

Fact: The infant mortality rate in the United States is worse than in 23 other industrialized countries. (6)

General Motors spent $3.4 billion on health coverage for its employees in 1991. That amounts to $929 for every car it built. The medical bill for a typical U.S. firm in 1991 averaged $3,605 per worker and equaled 45% of its after-tax profits. Guess what topic is hot in American boardrooms? (462, p. 89)

▪ If you think General Motors' situation is unique, think again. As a percentage of wages and salaries, business health care costs more than *doubled* between 1970 and 1987. How serious are health care costs for U.S. corporations? In 1987, employee health care costs paid by U.S. corporations were the equivalent of more than 94% of total after-tax corporate profits. (423, p. 8)

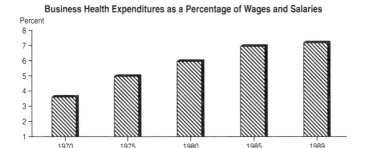

Business Health Expenditures as a Percentage of Wages and Salaries

Source: Health Care Financing Administration, Office of the Actuary; see Ref. 423, p. 1.

∎ As seen in the accompanying bar chart, business health spending grew more than eightfold between 1970 and 1987.

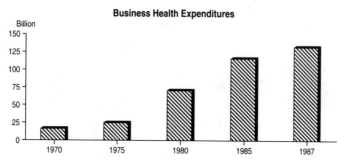

Business Health Expenditures

Source: Health Care Financing Administration, Office of the Actuary; see Ref. 423, p. 10.

====

About 18% of *all* part-time workers lack health insurance coverage from any source. (364, p. 22)

====

1/3 *One-third* of American workers remain without employer-provided insurance. (229, p. xv)

====

One of every seven Americans has·no medical coverage at all. (430)

====

∎ By the year 2030 the elderly will represent 22% of the U.S. population, up from 12% in 1990. (412)

====

Fallacy: Our population is aging, but we can handle the benefit programs for our elderly.

50% **Fact:** Let us hope we can, because if present benefit systems remain in effect, U.S. programs for the elderly could consume 50% of the federal budget by the year 2025. (9, p. 71)

 Ten percent of a Canadians' income goes to a tax fund for health care. Canadian patients pick their physicians, who charge the government for their services according to a fee schedule. Patients pay $200 for a routine delivery of a baby, a procedure that costs $1,500 in Kansas City. (27, p. 48)

Fallacy: Health insurance and the cost of actual medical treatment are the culprits in America's soaring health care costs.

 Fact: Combined, these expenditures cost health care consumers 12% of U.S. GNP. The average for other industrialized nations is only 7.5%. Administrative expenses account for half the difference. These expenses account for 30% of the U.S. health care bill, compared with 10% for our major competitor nations. (20)

Fallacy: With steady increases in nursing graduates and the decreasing number of bed patients, we will soon solve our nursing shortage.

Fact: This appears to be true, but according to management guru Peter Drucker, the reason for a continuing shortage of nurses is that half of their time is taken up by paperwork for Medicare, Medicaid, insurers, billing, and so on. How else can there be a shortage of nurses as the number of them has increased while the number of bed patients has decreased? (71, p. 74)

I'm OK, you're not OK! That must be the case, since 82% of Americans rate the health care they receive as good or excellent, but only 33% rate the quality of their country's health care system that high. (86)

Fallacy: Pharmaceutical companies are making money hand over fist.

Fact: Pharmaceutical companies spent an average of $231 million in research and development for each new drug developed during the 1980s. Seven of 10 drugs that made it to market never recovered this cost. (12, p. 56)

━━━

Fallacy: Maternity and paternity leaves are seldom offered to employees.

 Fact: An average *83%* of companies offer maternity leave. Of companies with fewer than 10 employees, 79% offer it; of companies with 50 or more employees, 84% offer it. Of all companies offering maternity leave, 67% continue health benefits. The percentage of the smallest and largest companies doing so is about the same. The length of maternity leave averages 11.3 weeks in companies with 50 or more employees. It averages 9.1 weeks in companies with fewer than 10 employees. Sixty percent of all companies offer paternity leave. (25, p. 28)

━━━

 Need a job? Try the health care field. Growth in health services has risen from 2.4% of gross national product in 1980 to approximately 12% in 1990, and the upward trend appears to be continuing despite government and private sector efforts to contain health care costs (according to a report by the U.S. Department of Commerce). (307)

━━━

 Fallacy: There is a serious risk of patients contracting AIDS from health care workers.

Fact: As of mid-1991, five Americans had contracted AIDS from a health care worker, but 40 health care workers had contracted AIDS from a patient. (85)

Fallacy: Normal body temperature for a healthy adult is 98.6 degrees Fahrenheit.

Fact: Carl Wunderlich based the 98.6 degree standard on more than 1 million temperature readings he took on 25,000 people in 1868. His findings were never seriously tested until a 1992 study was done more scientifically on 148 healthy men and women. This newer study found the average temperature to be 98.2 degrees Fahrenheit. The women in the sample averaged 98.4 degrees and the men averaged 98.1 degrees. Whoever said men were cold blooded may have been right. (189)

In 1991, 9,337,000 wisdom teeth were extracted from American mouths. (188) We can only hope it wasn't a dumb mistake.

Nothing cold or hot, waiter! There were 500 million unfilled cavities in the United States in 1990. (88)

Attention, G.I. shoppers, our blue light special for the day is . . . . The U.S. army bought 25,550 bottles of suntan lotion from one K-Mart store in Hinesville, Georgia, during the month of August 1990. The sun is pretty intense around Hinesville in August, I'll betcha. (88)

Forget the six million dollar man! There are now some 200 different artificial parts for the human body. A complete set costs $25,000,000. (188)

∎ Influenza is the most common cause of work-loss days.

∎ In 1991, 27% of Americans had one or more forms of heart disease, blood vessel disease, or high blood pressure.

———

∎ The most common inpatient surgical procedure is a cesarean section.

———

∎ One in eight Americans suffers from sinus infections—it surpasses arthritis as the most common chronic disease in the United States.

———

∎ We want to "pump you up." Company employees in poor physical shape have two and a half times the rate of absenteeism.

———

∎ One in five hospital beds is taken up by a person who has broken a hip.

———

∎ It is estimated that 87% of Americans have some form of periodontal (gum) disease.

———

∎ What pain? Studies indicate that 50% of heart attack victims wait more than two hours before getting to an emergency room.

———

∎ Work can be good for your health. Working women are at significantly less risk of heart disease than are nonemployed women.

Insurance

Fallacy: Businesses are very serious about holding down workers' compensation claims.

Fact: Not always. Most businesses insure their workers' compensation liabilities with an insurance company. Small businesses pay heavily for this insurance because their small number of employees mean a higher risk from the insuring company. But most larger businesses insure under a "cost-plus" arrangement. Ironically, such plans pay the insuring company more revenue for more claim losses filed. This gives them an incentive to file more, rather than fewer, claims—a reverse (perverse?) incentive!

Very large firms are usually self-insured. Many of them contract with a third-party administrator to handle the filing of claims. Here, again, these arrangements are usually cost plus, giving the third-party administrator the same reverse incentive.

These common arrangements for handling workers' compensation claims are convenient for businesses, but they increase costs that businessmen say they want to control. (115)

Fallacy: One benefit of the downsizing trend in U.S. companies is fewer workers' compensation claims because there are fewer employees.

Fact: A survey of 177 companies found that 55 of them cut their work forces during recent years. A third of these 55 companies said that the percentage of their downsized work forces filing workers' compensation claims rose. The reason for the added claims is that the remaining employees, many of whom are older workers, are doing unfamiliar jobs in which they are becoming injured. (153)

Fallacy: The sale of life insurance policies climbs in good times and bad because people always need this protection.

Fact: The sales volume of life insurance policies to individuals fell in 1991 for the first time in 42 years. That same year the number of new policies dropped 5% for the eighth consecutive year. (184, p. 46)

∎ Ignored groups: The American Council of Life Insurance identified a group of about 20 million people they call "new-collar" workers in the under-$50,000 market that is generally ignored by the financial services industry. They include data entry clerks, bank tellers, public utility workers, and state or civil service workers. (184, p. 48)

Fallacy: It's the manufacturers that really contribute to our gross national product (GNP).

Fact: The U.S. Bureau of Economic Analysis attempted to place a dollar value on the services rendered by the insurance industry. They estimated the insurance industry's contribution to the GNP at $101 billion in 1987. That compares to $49.9 billion for the automobile manufacturers. The banking industry's contribution was estimated to be $85 billion. (417, p. 3)

 If you put all the people employed in the U.S. insurance industry in one place you would create a city the size of Brooklyn. (417, p. 4)

Fallacy: It's the banks that hold all the capital.

Fact: At the end of 1990, Prudential Insurance Company had over $8 billion of capital. That was more than the combined capital of two of the nation's largest banks—Chase Manhattan and Banker's Trust. (180, p. 74)

Fallacy: Most employees don't rely on employer-provided life insurance to meet their financial needs because they know that they lose such protection if they lose their jobs.

Fact: The Voluntary Employee Benefits Board found that *70% of employees rely entirely on employer-provided life insurance.* They have little or no permanent coverage on themselves and no coverage on their dependents. (184, p. 48)

Less than half of small businesses with fewer than 10 employees offer health care insurance to their workers. (423, p. 3)

Most of the uninsured are employed. In 1985, more than 35 million people under age 65 in the United States did not have some form of health insurance coverage. (420, p. 2)

Over 65 million households are not being serviced by today's insurance agents. These include 52 million married couples earning between $35,000 and $49,000 per year and over 13 million single-parent households. (183, p. 14)

In 1991 the *New England Journal of Medicine* forecasted that 43% of Americans reaching age 65 will spend some time in nursing homes. Few within this group had insurance protection against the huge expense of long-term residence in a nursing home. (182, p. 46)

Fallacy: AIDS is now the greatest health-related underwriting risk for life insurers.

Fact: This may become true later, but not yet. *Alcohol abuse is a* *greater risk.* An estimated 10.5 million Americans are alcohol dependent, and more than 7 million of them are alcohol abusers. Each year about 200,000 American deaths are directly related to alcohol abuse. By contrast, the *total* number of reported deaths from AIDS through July 1991 was 118,411. (185, p. 46)

Fallacy: With all the risks to life and income in today's fast-paced life in America, sales of life insurance policies to young adults should be booming.

Fact: Maybe they should be booming, but they are not. Sales of first-time life policies as a proportion of all policies fell from a high of 33% in 1984 to 26% in 1991. In fact, fewer life policies of all types were sold in 1991 than in 1980. Reasons for the declining sales include fewer agents, fewer good prospects (those married with children), and an increase in nonlife insurance retirement/investment vehicles. (186, p. 100)

Fallacy: Economic recessions and job loss cause just about all mortgage foreclosures.

Fact: Homeowners suffering *disabilities* cause 48% of mortgage foreclosures. (187, p. 168)

Jobs and Employment

Fallacy: I don't work in the auto industry, so what happens in it is not important to me.

Fact: Want to know why the troubled American auto is of concern to Americans? Consider that *one of every seven U.S. jobs* is related to the auto industry. The employees who hold these jobs pay *one of every eight tax dollars.* (141, p. 83)

Fallacy: Companies get in trouble more often for bias involving race or sex than for anything else involving the work force.

Fact: As of 1989, the U.S. Equal Employment Opportunity Commission (EEOC) said employers paid about $9 million in back compensation and damages in EEOC cases brought under Title VII of the Civil Rights Act. Surprisingly, during that period, employers paid out about *$25 million* in EEOC cases involving violations of the *Age Discrimination in Employment Act.* The same ratio holds true for bias suits brought by private attorneys. It is age discrimination that gets most companies in trouble. (442)

Fallacy: The United States faces a labor shortage in the 1990s.

Fact: Human resource specialists have predicted this since at least as far back as 1978. It seemed to be a sure bet, based on demographic trends that show that we will have 15.6 million new workers by the year 2000. Assuming a moderate GNP growth rate of 2.9%, we will have 23.8 million jobs by then. Where will we find the people? (376)

But economic events have intervened, causing some economists now to predict far slower growth in the labor force and a possible labor surplus by the turn of the century. The problem is slower job creation and continued downsizing within larger firms. The *Fortune* 500 companies, for example, employed 3.7 million fewer workers in 1991 than they did in 1981. That represents a whopping 25% job reduction among those firms, and few forecasters expect much rehiring after the early 1990s recession ends. (143, pp. 64–65)

───

Fallacy: There will be a labor surplus by the year 2000.

Fact: We just said that in the last fact, didn't we? But that was a combined forecast for all types of jobs. By the year 2000, there are likely to be too few *well-educated* and *well-trained* workers to satisfy the nation's economic need. This is the opinion of the U.S. Department of Labor Employment & Training Administration. (248, p. 1)

───

 Between 1985 and 2000, more than 600 million new job seekers will be added to the world's work force. (217, p. 13)

───

■ In mid-1992, the European Economic Community (EC) had 40% of the work force in the industrialized world, but 60% of its unemployed workers. One prediction sees Europe's share of the jobless rising to 80% by the decade's end. The reason is that European firms were laying off huge numbers of workers to restructure themselves for the stiffer competition coming as the EC planned to open its borders on January 1, 1993. (174, p. 45)

───

■ Between now and the year 2000, the U.S. work force will grow more slowly than at any time since the 1930s. It will rise only 1% per year during this period. (221, p. 6)

Fallacy: High-technology jobs will be the fastest-growing segment of the U.S. economy during the next 15 years.

Fact: Many types of jobs will include the use of high-tech equipment in the future. Still, we will not be thinking of paralegals, personal and home care aids, physical therapists, medical assistants, and human service positions as high-tech jobs. Those are the ones the Bureau Labor Statistics forecasts will grow the fastest between 1990 and 2005. (49, p. 54)

 Each year about *1 million* U.S. workers lose their jobs because of business closures and permanent layoffs. On average, dislocated workers remain unemployed for 14 weeks with an estimated productivity loss of almost $4,500 per worker or a total loss to the U.S. economy of about $9 billion per year. (424, p. 10)

50% Half of all workers hired between 1988 and 2000 will be minorities. (264, p. 103)

Fallacy: Most workers in the United States have been here a long time.

Fact: The Federal Immigration and Naturalization Service estimated that about *one in four* workers entering the American labor force between the mid-1980s and the year 2000 will be immigrants. (20, p. 216)

 Between 1980 and 1987, 22% of the growth in the U.S. labor force consisted of immigrants. That is more than twice the percentage during the 1970s. (117, p. 48)

Fallacy: Having young children keeps few mothers out of the work force.

Fact: The lack of affordable, quality child care was the reason an estimated 1.1 million mothers did not seek or hold a job in 1986, according to two articles in the *Monthly Labor Review,* published by the Bureau of Labor Statistics. The average weekly expenditures on child care ranged from about $45 for older mothers to about $60 for younger mothers (in 1988 dollars). (218, p. 2)

 The revised fourth edition of the *Dictionary of Occupational Titles* for 1991 shows 2000 new or changed occupations since the last edition, which was published 14 years ago. When this dictionary was first published in 1939, it included jobs for button reclaimers, dance floor attendants, egg smellers, and rag workers. Changes in the new dictionary reflect changes in society. There are more service and fewer industrial jobs. But are all our changes for the best? In 1939, you could not get a job as a stress-test technician; now you can. (219, p. 5)

 Princeton economist Alan Krueger estimates that if you take two otherwise equally skilled employees, the one who can use a computer can earn 15% more. (143, p. 74)

 Believe it or not, it is possible to shop for a job while you shop for your clothes—at least in some parts of the country. In two malls in Virginia, computers with up-to-date listings of more than 21,000 jobs have been installed. Looking for a job? Push a button on a computer screen and an automated voice guides you through the steps as you select job classifications and locations.

The system is called ALEX (Automated Labor Exchange), and it can be found in job service offices and veteran outreach centers in a six-state region that includes Maryland, Virginia,

Delaware, West Virginia, and the District of Columbia as well as in the two earlier-mentioned Virginia malls. It was developed with an $815,000 grant from the U.S. Labor Department to improve employment service. (216, p. 3)

∎ The Bureau of Labor Statistics estimates that 2.8 million manufacturing workers lost their jobs during the 1980s. One-third of them were hired into service jobs paying 20% less. (20, pp. 215–216)

 The rich get richer. The average income of the richest fifth of American families rose about 9% between 1977 and 1990, while the poorest fifth became about 7% poorer. (20, p. 197)

---

1 in 4 There is a 25% chance that an African-American male below the age of 25 years living in Los Angeles is unemployed. (42) No wonder there were riots.

∎ There have been close relationships between losses and gains in temporary jobs and losses and gains in regular jobs for over a decade. After a lag of one or two months, each gain or decline of 50,000 temporary jobs predicts a shift of 1 million payroll jobs in the same direction. (137)

Fallacy: Defense workers laid off after the collapse of communism in 1989–1991 can go to work for commercial companies as defense money is transferred to civilian purposes.

Fact: Only about 15% of defense workers have skills that they can easily transfer to commercial businesses. Many other workers have skills too specialized to transfer easily, and *half* of defense employees do paperwork and support jobs monitoring contract and hiring rules. (143, p. 65)

Fallacy: Most scientists and engineers will be hired by manufacturers.

Fact: Three-fifths of the projected increase in science and engineering jobs will be in the service-producing industries. (434)

Fallacy: Most new jobs will require a college degree.

Fact: About 60% of the new jobs between 1985 and 2000 will be in technical fields requiring more than a high school education but less than a four-year college degree. (435)

Legal

If you put all the U.S. lawyers in one place (why not?), you would have a crowd as large as the population of Hartford, Connecticut, or about 756,000. If current law school students graduate, there will be 1 lawyer for every 290 Americans by 1995. Don't get mad, sue! (290)

Fallacy: Japan employs about the same number of staff professionals as we do in the United States

Fact: Japan has 1 lawyer for every 20 in the United States, 3 accountants for every 40 in the United States, *but* 400 engineers for every 20 in the United States (21, p. 16)

Fastest justice in the East? Ninety-nine out of 100 defendants tried in criminal cases in Japan are found guilty. (188)

Fallacy: Firing an employee ends the employee's compensation from the employer.

Fact: Wrongful discharge suits to individual employees have exceeded the $1 million mark in some states. In 1986, plaintiffs received favorable verdicts in 78% of wrongful-discharge cases that went to California juries, and the average award was $424,527. (321)

In 1980, corporations faced a 1 in 15 chance that their corporate income tax return would be audited. The chances dropped to 1 in 39 by 1992. (86)

In the mid-1980s, product liability cost increases were so large (as much as 1,000%) that some businesses could no longer afford such insurance. As a result, some aircraft manufacturers stopped producing many types of general aviation aircraft, all U.S. manufacturers of trampolines stopped production, and some pharmaceutical firms stopped research on new drugs. (432, p. 10)

It is estimated that 42% of the amounts paid by defendants in tort cases is for legal fees and expenses. (432, p. 48)

Justice is swift? The U.S. government's General Accounting Office found that it usually takes several years to resolve product liability cases. The trial process was relatively short (about four-tenths of a month, or 12 days) from the start of the trial to the verdict. However, the average time leading up to the trial was about 30 months. (432, p. 49)

Made in America

Fallacy: It's easy to know what's made in America.

Fact: General Motors owns about 34% of Isuzu and 5% of Suzuki. Ford owns 25% of Mazda Motors. Chrysler owns 24% of Mitsubishi. (336, p. 6)

———

 Honda, a Toyota or a Nissan—about 40% of the cars sold with these nameplates in the United States are *made in America.* (427)

———

WHAT'S AMERICAN?
SOMETIMES IT'S TOUGH TO TELL

The recent buy-America binge has raised the question of just which common products are, in fact, made by American companies. Here's a quiz:

1. The parent company of Braun household appliances is
   a. Swiss   b. German   c. American   d. Japanese

2. Bic pens are
   a. Japanese   b. Czech   c. American   d. French

3. The maker of Häagen-Dazs ice cream is based in
   a. France   b. Sweden   c. Britain   d. America

4. RCA televisions are made by a company based in
   a. Japan   b. America   c. France   d. Korea

5. The parent of Green Giant vegetables is
   a. German   b. Italian   c. American   d. British

6. Godiva chocolate is
   a. French   b. Belgian   c. Swiss   d. American

7. Vaseline's owner is
   a. American   b. French   c. Anglo-Dutch d. German

8. Wrangler jeans are
   a. American   b. French   c. Korean   d. Canadian

9. Holiday Inns are owned by a company based in
   a. France   b. America   c. Britain   d. Saudi Arabia

10. Tropicana orange juice is owned by a company based in
    a. Brazil   b. Canada   c. Mexico   d. America

Answers:

1. c (Gillette Co.)
2. d (Bic SA)
3. c (Grand Metropolitan PLC)
4. c (Thomson SA)
5. d (Grand Metropolitan PLC)
6. d (Campbell Soup Co.)
7. c (Unilever PLC)
8. d (VF Corp.)
9. c (Bass PLC)
10. b (Seagram Co. Ltd)

Courtesy of Wisconsin State Journal; *see Ref. 428.*

───

Fallacy: Buying an American car keeps jobs in America.

Fact: In 1991, Ford reduced the domestic content of the Ford Crown Victoria and Mercury Grand Marquis from *94% to 73%.* Ford ships parts to the plant in *Hermosillo, Mexico,* that makes the Mercury Tracer. It is not always clear what is and what is not made in America. Honda Accord makes *75%* of the car's parts in the United States, but only about 25% are actually made by American-owned companies. Japanese suppliers based in the United States make the rest. (14)

Fallacy: Made in America means it is made in America.

Fact: Not always. Consider the international transactions involved when one buys a $20,000 Pontiac Le Mans:

▪ $6,000 to South Korea for routine labor and assembly

▪ $3,500 to Japan for advanced components (engines, transaxles, and electronics)

▪ $1,500 to West Germany for styling and design engineering

▪ $800 to Taiwan, Singapore, and Japan for small components

▪ $500 to Great Britain for advertising and marketing services

▪ About $100 to Ireland and Barbados for data processing

▪ Less than $8,000 to strategists in Detroit, lawyers and bankers in New York, lobbyists in Washington, insurance and health care workers all over the country, and General Motors shareholders (many of whom are foreign nationals) (20, p. 113)

Ah, the good ol' days. In 1930 fewer than 50,000 cars traveled the roads of Japan, and 94% of them were made in America. (383, p. 14)

By 1960, U.S. autoworkers made about half the cars in the world; now we make about 20%. The car capital of the world is Toyota City, not Detroit. (384)

▪ Significant portions of many large companies' assets and employees are outside their home country. Some examples from 1989:

	Percentage of Total Assets Outside Home Country	Percentage of Total Number of Employees Outside Home Country
IBM	46%	44%
General Motors	24%	31%
DuPont	35%	24%
General Electric	9%	17%

Source: Computed from company annual reports; U.S. Department of Commerce, Survey of Current Business, June 1990.

Think that is bad?

Switzerland's Nestlé has 95% of its assets and 96.5% of its employees located outside its home nation. (378, p. 109)

———

Fallacy: American-made steel is better than Japanese-made steel.

Fact: Only 8% of American steel buyers rated American steel "excellent," while 60% rated Japanese steel "excellent." (90)

———

Fallacy: Airbus Industrie has gained market share against U.S. aircraft manufacturers Boeing and McDonnell Douglas by getting government subsidies that let Airbus charge a lower price for its commercial jets. *U.S. firms get no government subsidies.*

Fact: A U.S. Commerce Department study estimates that Airbus received $26 billion in subsidies through 1989 from the four countries with an interest in the firm—France, Germany, Britain, and Spain. It is true that the two U.S. firms get no direct government subsidies. But Airbus commissioned a study that showed its U.S. competitors received between $33 billion and $41 billion of indirect aid from the U.S. government. These indirect subsidies came in the form of tax incentives and spillover technology from NASA and defense contracts. (66, pp. 103–104)

∎ In 1979, 94% of the computers bought in the United States were made here; in 1989, that figure was 66%. (22, p. 62)

———

Fallacy: Most semiconductors used in America are made in Japan. (Ross Perot asserted this during his 1992 presidential campaign.)

Fact: Not so. U.S. producers make 70% of the semiconductors used in the United States, while the Japanese make less than 20% of them. (285)

———

∎ When we think of high-quality leather shoes, most think Italian. Well, some of the most popular leather shoes in Italy have a "Made in America" label. (228)

Manufacturing Competitiveness

Fallacy: America is or has been a *manufacturing economy.*

Fact: Manufacturing employment currently represents 16–17% of the labor force; it has *never* exceeded 27% (since the first available statistics in 1840). (330)

In the last 15 years, foreign producers have doubled their penetration of the U.S. market for manufactured goods, increasing their percentage of sales from 6% to 12%. (261, p. 2)

The U.S. General Accounting Office estimates that the production of Japanese-affiliated automakers in the United States led to about 11,000 net job losses in 1989. This compares to 25,000 net jobs lost in 1988. The reason that not as many jobs were lost in 1989 as in 1988 was the reported increased use of U.S. parts (from 28% in 1988 to 50% in 1989).

In 1989, Japanese-affiliated automakers' production in the United States provided 66,000 jobs but displaced 77,000 other jobs; there is the 11,000 net job loss. Of this 11,000, direct factory jobs decreased by an estimated 1,000 due to the greater labor efficiency of Japanese automakers when compared to General Motors, Ford, and Chrysler. The remaining 10,000 lost jobs were upstream supplier jobs. These suppliers provide inputs directly or indirectly to the vehicles up to the point of assembly. (371, pp. 1–2)

Fallacy: European auto manufacturers have become the industrialized world's least efficient car producers.

Fact: Some say so, but they were doing something about it on the eve of opening their borders to competition from one another and from Japanese and American competitors at the beginning of 1993. As one example, France's Peugeot raised its productivity a whopping 50% from 1988 to 1992. General Motors admits that it must lower the average production costs of its European-built cars $1,000 to compete in the future. (174, p. 44)

Fallacy: The United States' share of the world's manufacturing output is declining.

Fact: At about 32%, the U.S. share of the world's manufacturing is about where it was in 1913 and 1938 (before the two world wars). The U.S. decrease in share that began in the 1950s was seen as an indicator that the United States had succeeded in helping allies rebuild economies devastated by World War II. (385, p. 56)

Fallacy: U.S. manufacturing productivity is in critical condition.

Fact: U.S. manufacturers' productivity is the world's highest. It grew faster in the late 1980s than did West Germany's productivity, and it grew less than a percentage point slower than did Japan's rate during the 1980s. (270)

Fallacy: America is losing manufacturing jobs around the world.

Fact: America's share of manufacturing jobs in the United States, Japan, Europe, and the newly industrializing countries was 27% in 1960, 30% in 1980, and still 30% in 1986. Europe's share of these jobs fell from 51% in 1960 to 32% in 1986. During this period, manufacturing jobs within the United States fell from 34% to 24% of U.S. jobs, while service jobs rose from 56% to 73% of the total. True, the United States lost manufacturing jobs within the United States, but not outside its borders. (19, p. 153)

───

Fallacy: The level of competition in the global auto market has peaked and is leveling out.

 Fact: The level of competitiveness continues to rise. Japan's automakers aim to *build and deliver* new models—in the buyer's choice of color and options—in just *three days.* (206, p. 66)

───

Fallacy: General Motors' alliance with Toyota in the former's Fremont, California, plant has helped GM learn how to build a more competitive small car.

Fact: Apparently not. Ten years after this GM/Toyota alliance began, the Toyota car made in this plant outsells GM's version 6 to 1. (193, p. 50)

───

Fallacy: Better cars come from highly automated plants.

Fact: That doesn't hold true for General Motors. In its just-mentioned Fremont, California, plant, GM uses less automation than the average auto plant, but some say the cars built in that plant are of higher quality than those from GM's most highly automated plant. (315, p. 791)

───

Fallacy: Most of the time and money spent on manufacturing goods is spent on the actual manufacturing process.

Fact: It's not even close! *Eighty percent* or more of total time needed to produce a product, its components, and subassemblies does not involve the actual production process. Almost all the cost associated with manufactured items is for moving them, storing them, and waiting to work on them. Some estimates for this nonmanufacturing time exceed *90%* of total manufacturing time. (297)

Fallacy: To speed present products to market, we must speed the manufacturing process.

Fact: Philip Thomas, president of Thomas Group, says that manufacturing often takes only 5–10% of the time to fill an order and get a product to market. The rest of the time is administrative. (35, p. 56)

Motorola starts producing one of its custom-built pocket pagers within 17 minutes after receiving an order and ships the product within 2 hours. The customer receives the pager the next day. (315, p. 799)

By 1995 many factories will have no direct labor operators. This prediction was made by Bill Wiggenhorn, president of Motorola University and corporate vice president of Training and Education at Motorola, Inc. (392, p. 1)

We think that operating a manufacturing plant at 70% of its capacity is very low. But managers at Fujitsu Fanuc, the Japanese robot manufacturer, say their firm can *break even at 20%* capacity utilization and can make profits on exports with a currency as strong as 70 yen to the dollar. Tough competition! (19, p. 35)

In 1977, foreigners owned about 3.5% of America's manufacturing capacity. By 1990, they had more than 11%. They also employed 10% of the U.S. work force. (1, p. 6)

A quarter of American manufacturing workers continue to be covered by collective bargaining agreements, compared to less than 10% in many service industries. (240, p. 236)

Fallacy: Union strikes are a major cause of lowered economic growth in the United States.

Fact: Strikes have never been a serious drag on the U.S. economy, especially not during recent years. The number of strikes fell 79% from 1980 to 1992. (161)

Fallacy: The Japanese are taking the data storage technology that we invented and then improving the production method to cut prices and capture market share.

 Fact: In *today's* data storage technology—disk drives—yes. But American companies lead in *tomorrow's* storage technology called *flash memory.*

Flash memory consists of silicon chips that will retain stored data even when a computer's power is turned off. They are faster, smaller, lighter, more accurate, and cheaper than today's hard disk drives. The brief history of flash memory is interesting because it is the exact reverse of most stories of new technologies that are invented in America and then taken over by the Japanese.

Toshiba, a Japanese firm, invented flash memory. Intel, an American Company, improved Toshiba's design and production methods and then cut the price drastically. Intel now has 85% of the fast-growing world flash memory market, and Advanced Micro Devices, another U.S. firm, ranks second. Major Japanese firms are struggling to compete. Some of them are complaining that Intel is dumping (selling below cost) and threaten to bring a lawsuit against the firm. U.S. computer technology lives! (59, p. D2)

In 1991, the question posed to 25 American executives by Grant Thornton, the accounting firm, was *"When you think of U.S. manufacturers with top quality standards, which one company comes to mind?"* The companies listed on the next page came up the most often, but the most frequent answer was *"none"!* (440, p. 8)

1. IBM
2. Ford
3. Motorola
4. Hewlett-Packard
5. General Motors
6. Xerox
7. Cadillac
8. General Electric
9. 3M
10. Apple Computer

Fallacy: A major reason for Japan's manufacturing competitiveness is the lower cost of capital available to Japanese manufacturers.

Fact: True for many years, but no longer. The Japanese have been able to borrow at interest rates as low as 2% in the past. But the collapse of the Japanese stock market in 1991 and 1992 and higher interest rates caused the cost of capital to rise to 5.6% by mid–1992. That equals the cost for U.S. business. (141, p. 83)

Marketing

Fallacy: It's the small companies that serve a market niche.

Fact: Mass market appeal? Seventy-five percent of respondents to a survey of *Fortune* 1000 firms said their companies have started serving smaller segments for at least some of their products and services. (360, p. 43)

Fallacy: One customer is just as important as the next.

Fact: A small percentage of your customers may purchase very large percentages of your product. For example, airlines found that 4.1% of adults made 70.4% of all airline trips. (360, p. 44)

Expectant sales? Huggies spent over $10 million on a system that gives its marketers the names of more than three-fourths of U.S. expectant mothers. Why? The average baby who uses disposable diapers consumes $1,400 of them each year. (92, p. 17)

Ninety-five percent of the food advertised on Saturday morning TV is junk food. (85)

■ Crystal Pepsi taste testers prefer traditional brown colas to the newer clear cola. This is not too surprising when you consider that they tested 3,000 versions of Crystal Pepsi before introducing the new drink to the market! (148)

Fallacy: Americans are loyal to their brand of soft drink.

Fact: Ray Charles says "Uh huh" (in Pepsi commercials), but we say "uh uh"! Only 60% of soft drink consumers say they are strongly committed to their brand. (161)

■ There are an estimated 32,000 Tupperware parties and demonstrations worldwide each day. (161)

 G. Heileman introduced a high-alcohol-content malt liquor (5.9%) named Colt 45 Premium and is test marketing it in low-income neighborhoods. It's the same group that markets Black Hat (formerly Black Death) vodka. (12, p 5)

 Old man Michelin. The chubby and cute Michelin Man seems like a fairly new corporate symbol to us in the United States. The fact is, the French-owned tire company has used this fella as a corporate symbol since 1898. A pile of rubber tires inspired his creator. (110, p. 154)

Fallacy: Market research is too expensive for small and mid-sized companies.

Fact: Good market research does not have to be expensive, as a 1992 survey of small and medium-sized firms conducted by *Inc.* magazine and The Executive Committee shows. The study found that customers are the best source of market research for new products and services. Nearly 40% of the 173 chief executive officers surveyed spent less than $1,000 on a market research project. (192)

Nuke it! Half of college students say they use a microwave oven every day. Half of them say their favorite food is pizza. (280)

Fallacy: Marketers are targeting the growing consumer spending by Hispanics in the United States.

Fact: Not yet. DRI/McGraw-Hill estimates that Hispanics now spend about $200 billion a year in the United States, yet only 1% of advertising budgets are focused on them. (445, p. 30)

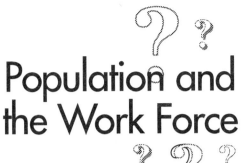

Population and the Work Force

 What would the world be like if it were reduced to a village of 1,000 people? The World Development Forum says the village would contain 564 Asians, 210 Europeans, 86 Africans, 80 South Americans, and 60 North Americans. There would be 300 Christians (183 Catholics, 84 Protestants, 33 Orthodox), 175 Muslims, 128 Hindus, 55 Buddhists, 47 Animists (spirit worshippers), 85 representing other religious groups, and 210 atheists. Sixty of the villagers would have half the total income, 500 would be hungry, 600 would live in shantytowns, and 700 would be illiterate. (120, p. 6)

Fallacy: Now that the cold war is over, the main economic threat to richer nations from poor nations is an influx of products from these poor nations.

Fact: The wealthy nations wish that were the main threat. The bigger threat is an influx of *people* from poor nations. The United Nations reports that 75 million people move from country to country each year in search of work. The end of the cold war will make this movement easier. (56, p. A1)

■ Times, they are a changin'. More people identify themselves as Hispanic than identify themselves as African Americans in 19 states. (42)

Immigrants from Latin America and Asia accounted for one-fifth of America's population growth in the 1980s. (266, p. 114)

Fallacy: The tidal wave of immigrants into the United States during recent years is placing too heavy a burden on our welfare system.

Fact: About 11 million immigrants are working in the United States. They earn about $240 billion a year, from which they pay over $90 billion in taxes. This far exceeds the estimated $5 billion that immigrants get in welfare payments. (131, p. 114)

Fallacy: Too high a proportion of immigrants to the United States have little education, so they will not help the United States develop the knowledge-based economy it needs for the future.

Fact: About one-fourth of immigrants working in the United States are college graduates, a slightly greater proportion than for native Americans. For several years to come, most of the scientists and engineers in America's high-tech companies will be immigrants. (131, pp. 116, 117)

Fallacy: All these immigrants coming to the United States are hurting our competitiveness.

Fact: Consider these facts:

∎ Half of all U.S. engineering Ph.D.s are now awarded to immigrants.

∎ Over 10,000 highly trained Asian immigrants are employees in the electronic and computer industry.

∎ Immigrant workers have a higher rate of starting new businesses than do American-born workers—9.2% versus 7.1%. (443)

Fallacy: African Americans feel particularly resentful toward immigrants.

Fact: A *Business Week*/Harris poll taken in mid-1992 revealed that African Americans generally feel more positive toward immigrants than do non–African Americans. (131, p. 119)

 America is not the only country dealing with immigrants. Immigrants make up almost 5% of the West European population. Foreign-born children comprise over 10% of primary school enrollment in France, Germany, and Sweden. From 5 million to 9 million more people are expected to immigrate to Western Europe between 1992 and 1997. (133, p. 97)

Fallacy: The U.S. population is becoming the oldest of any industrialized nation.

 Fact: In 1980, Japan was the world's youngest industrial society; by 2000, it will be the oldest. Japan's population is aging twice as fast as West Germany's and six times faster than that of the United States. (9, p. 71)

 Fallacy: There is not enough food to feed a starving world population. Parts of the world will soon run out of food.

Fact: Despite famines in parts of Africa and elsewhere in the world, global food supplies are growing faster than demand, according to "Workforce 2000: Is Corporate America Prepared?", a U.S. Labor Department study prepared for the U.S. Congress. Production in both the developed and developing world grew at a compound rate of 2.4% annually between 1971 and 1986, compared with world population growth of 1.9%. (219, p. 6)

The world's level of economic output increased more than 12 times between 1900 and 1987, but the inflation-adjusted prices for ore, farm goods, and other primary products are lower now than in 1900. (5, p. 119)

Some estimate that global population grew at a 14% rate between 1000 and 1750 A.D. The same proportionate growth is now reached in fewer than eight years. (5, p. 115) The United Nations estimates world population more than tripled between 1900 and 1987.

World population rose above 5 billion in 1990. It is expected to reach 8 billion by 2025 and 16 billion by the year 2100. Each hour, 12,000 children are born. Sixty percent of them join families whose annual per person incomes are less than $350. (1, p. 307)

Fallacy: The world's population is shifting to today's big, industrialized democracies where they can find jobs and freedom.

Fact: Global population is shifting *away from* current industrialized democracies. Two of the top 5 and 7 of the top 20 countries by population were industrial democracies in 1950. Together they accounted for almost one-fourth of the big-country total. But by 1985, only 1 of the top 5, and 6 of the top 20 countries were industrial democracies, and they made up less than one-sixth of this group's total population. By 2025 only the United States among industrial democracies is projected to be in the top five. Only the United States and Japan will be among the top 20. (5, pp. 127–128) (It would be nice if these two countries by then were not economic and/or military adversaries.)

Politics and Business

Fallacy: The Democrats are the party of unions.

Fact: If they are, they are keeping it quiet. The word "union" does not appear in the text of the party's 1992 platform. (161)

Fallacy: The Republican Party does not create industrial policies for the United States. It relies instead on free market forces to guide investment.

Fact: This is more true during recent years, but we don't need to look back very far to see a different party. The Eisenhower administration built the federal interstate highway system in the 1950s. It also speeded the postwar growth of U.S. defense industries. (164, p. 109)

Fallacy: With the Republican Party's big-business image, most millionaire senators are Republicans.

Fact: There were 28 millionaires in the U.S Senate in 1992; 21 of them were Democrats. (188)

Fallacy: The economy and the stock market, in particular, prospers when the Republicans are in charge and suffers when the Democratic Party is in charge.

Fact: If you look at stock market performance during Republican and Democratic regimes as a barometer, you find that the facts don't support this widely believed assertion. Since 1921, Republicans have been in charge for 39 years and Democrats for 32 years. The stock market produced an average annual return of 11.6% during the years of Republican rule and 14.1% while the Democrats were in charge. Statisticians assert that the 2.5-per-centage-point difference is not statistically significant. (129)

Fallacy: The Republican Party is the party that is good for the economy.

Fact: There are many ways to judge this enduring bit of conventional wisdom; however, one fact we found questions its validity. The average increase in the U.S. gross national product during each four-year Democratic administration since 1949 is 20%, while it was 9% during each four-year Republican administration. (148)

∎ In 1989, the Pentagon spent $1,868.15 for each spare toilet seat cover for the C-5B cargo plane. We thought you ought to be "privy" to this fact. (188)

∎ "Here's the deal." During Ross Perot's candidacy in the 1992 presidential campaign, some joked about his being able to pay off the national debt with his personal money. In reality, if he used his wealth to pay the interest on the national debt, *he would be broke in 5.7 days.* (148)

Fallacy: The Federal Reserve can help an incumbent U.S. president's election campaign during a weak economy by lowering interest rates to stimulate the economy.

Fact: The Fed does have the power to lower the Federal Reserve discount rate to member banks, which usually results in lower interest rates. But the Fed uses extreme caution in exercising this power in the latter stages of a presidential campaign. One reason for the Fed's timidity is that lowering interest rates a short time before an election reemphasizes the economy's weakness, and that could be harmful to the incumbent. The Fed has never lowered interest rates during the month preceding a presidential election since the end of World War II. (457)

Fallacy: Lowering the capital gains tax would stimulate the U.S. economy.

Fact: Not much, according to two simulation studies. One found that eliminating this tax would result in only a 0.06% rise in gross domestic product (GDP). The other simulation found that the growth in GDP fostered by a 40% cut in the tax evaporated in less than two years. (460, p. 79)

━━━━━

Fallacy: Cutting the marginal tax rate on individual incomes will encourage savings and investment by raising the after-tax return on investments.

Fact: Good theory, but it didn't work in the 1980s because people didn't save more when their marginal tax rates were cut. (460, p. 80)

━━━━━

Fallacy: Americans who live out a normal life span will get back from Social Security, Medicare, and other entitlement programs about the amount that they paid into the federal treasury during their working years.

Fact: Using a method called generational accounting, economist Lawrence Kotlikoff calculates that the present value of the difference between what a 35-year-old male will pay in taxes over his lifetime and the benefits he will receive is $195,000 in the government's favor. (461, p. 86)

━━━━━

Fallacy: The Democratic Party is the party of labor; the Republicans are favored by corporate managers.

Fact: Of course, there are many ways to judge this. But, if money talks, as many believe it does, then you might consider that corporations donate *three times* as much to the Democratic Party as do labor unions. (42)

━━━━━

Fallacy: In America, men are more interested in politics than women are.

Fact: It did not appear so in 1988, a year in which 7 million more women than men voted. (452)

Productivity

When 4,000 executives were asked by the Council for Competitiveness about U.S. competitiveness, 92% said they believed it was declining. (393)

Fallacy: We (the United States) used to be more productive than we are today.

Fact: Economist Juliet B. Schor examined our past and present work habits. She reports that the average American is *twice as productive* now as in 1948. (359, p. 10)

While we are more than twice as productive as in 1948, it is not enough! Throughout the postwar era, U.S. productivity has grown more slowly than that of its chief trading competitors. Between 1950 and 1983, output per hour of U.S. workers rose 129%. Productivity of Canadian workers rose 215%, that of French workers rose 458%, West Germans increased 508%, while Japanese workers increased their output a whopping 1,624%. *But things are getting better,* as seen in the following facts. (222, p. 5)

Fallacy: The U.S. worker is the world's most productive; German workers rank second, and the Japanese are third. The fears of the United States losing its competitive lead are overstated.

Fact: The first part of that statement is fact, but the second part is fallacy. While American workers *are* the most productive in the world, those in Germany and Japan are rapidly closing the gap. Part of the reason is lagging investment in the United States. From 1987 to 1991, U.S. private nonresidential investment as a percentage of GDP was the lowest among the Group of Seven nations. It was only half of Japan's percentage in 1991. Some results of this underinvestment: Two-thirds of metal-forming machine tools in use in the United States are more than 10 years old, the typical U.S. machine tool is seven years older than in Japan, and the average age of capital equipment used in nonfinancial U.S. corporations is the highest since 1965—8.5 years old. (198, p. 55)

Fallacy: Based on the foregoing fact, the United States should invest as much as possible to replace its aged plant and equipment.

Fact: Ah, you should know by now never to rely on just one of our facts as the answer to a complex problem. That would make for simplistic solutions to complex problems, and for a book too short to command the price we wanted you to pay.

Before we decide what to invest in, we need to consider the potential returns on our investment. While we certainly need to invest in plant and equipment, the returns on research and development can be even greater, *eight times greater*, according to a study by Columbia University professor Frank Lichtenberg. And what about investing in worker training? Hector Ruiz of Motorola claims his company gets returns on its training investment as high as 30 to 1. (198, pp. 55–57)

Fallacy: Because American worker's productivity has not increased as quickly as that of other workers, people assume we have a serious productivity problem in manufacturing.

Fact: We have a serious *service* productivity problem. Manufacturing output per worker between 1955 and 1970 grew at a compound annual rate of 2% per year. But in services, it *fell,* causing the overall pattern of output per worker to slide to only 0.5%. In the 1970s, each worker in the service and trade sectors of our economy produced $10,000 of output. This compared to $13,000 in the manufacturing sector. By 1985 service workers were producing $28,000 each. But by then annual manufacturing output per worker had skyrocketed to $41,200. (223, p. 5)

Fallacy: American industry only began to experience productivity problems during the past decade.

Fact: Following an early post–World War II boom, U.S. productivity growth declined substantially during the 1960s through the 1980s. The sharpest drop came in 1965. Economists proclaim several theories for our slowed growth. These include declines in the rate of capital investment, increases in the number of young, inexperienced workers during the 1970s, and a slowdown in the shift of workers from agriculture to industry. (220, p. 7)

As a group, Japanese office employees work 225 hours—almost six weeks per year—more than American office workers. (47, p. 154)

Fallacy: American manufacturing employees work less than their foreign counterparts.

Fact: It is true that Japanese manufacturing workers do log more hours. They put in six weeks more every year than their U.S. counterparts, mostly by working six-day weeks and skipping most of their vacation time. But the average U.S. employee puts in *163* *more hours* a year than in 1970 and labors eight weeks longer than the Germans. (244) So U.S. problems are not due to a lack of effort by average workers.

─────

Fallacy: The Japanese are tireless workers.

Fact: True, they work hard, but there is a price to be paid. A majority of adults surveyed complain of fatigue and emotional stress. In a survey when Japanese were asked if they usually feel tired, 11% said they felt very tired, and 53% said they felt somewhat tired. In the same survey 53% said they felt stress.

How hard do they work? The average Japanese employee in 1990 worked 2,044 hours, including 185 hours of overtime. That is 51 40-hour weeks a year. Americans worked 1,949 hours, or fewer than 49 40-hour weeks, or about $1\frac{1}{2}$ hours less per week than the Japanese. (247)

─────

Fallacy: It's our U.S. labor force that is causing our productivity and competitiveness problems.

Fact: Quasar, a Matsushita subsidiary, purchased a television plant from an American company several years ago. The results were amazing. In the American television manufacturing industry, the average defect rate is about 150 defects for every 100 sets built. Quasar achieved a defect rate of 15, or 10 times better than the U.S. average. But here is the really amazing part: It achieved that impressive quality record with the same American labor force used by the former owners. (313)

─────

Fallacy: American businesses have twice as many managers as do Japanese firms.

Fact: How about over *three times* as many? One of every 8 American workers is a manager or administrator, while only *1 of every 27* Japanese workers is. (161)

─────

Fallacy: U.S. manufacturing workers made modest earnings gains during the economic growth years of the 1980s.

Fact: When their wages are adjusted for inflation, these workers had *modest losses* during those years, according to the Labor Department. Their average hourly pay, including fringe benefits, fell from $14.89 in 1980 to $14.31 in 1989. Furthermore, one estimate shows that 43% of new jobs in 1979 included pensions and 23% of them offered health benefits. Only 38% of new jobs included pensions, and only 15% offered medical care by 1988. (143, p. 63)

#1

Fallacy: Japan is more productive than the United States.

Fact: The American worker is *number 1* when measuring productivity (output of goods and services per employed person). American workers' overall productivity is 30% higher than that of their Japanese counterparts and 28% higher than Japanese manufacturing workers' productivity. (357, p. 50)

Fallacy: U.S. productivity in manufacturing, farming, mining, construction, and transportation should continue to rise at about 3–4% a year, which is the 120-year historic average.

Fact: This average growth rate is likely to *fall soon* because fewer people are doing these kinds of work. There will be too few to have much effect on the rate of productivity growth. (72, p. 97)

Fallacy: Downsizing, rightsizing, and restructuring increase productivity.

Fact: Not always! In fact, it seems that about *half the time* productivity does not increase. In more than half of the 1,468 restructured companies surveyed by the Society for Human Resource Management, productivity either stayed the same or deteriorated after the layoffs. In another survey by a Philadelphia outplacement firm, 74% of senior managers at recently downsized companies said their workers had low morale, feared future cutbacks, and distrusted management. (232)

Working harder, not smarter! The Wyatt Company polled 1,005 corporations that employed over 4 million people. Most of these companies (86%) had downsized in the past five years, and over half (58%) had increased the amount of work that their employees had to do. (373)

———

 Depending on the industry, up to 40% of productivity in U.S. manufacturing and service companies is lost to rework. The corresponding *Japanese figure is 1–2%*. This statement comes from Larry Stern, a staff member of Pennsylvania Congressman Don Ritters. Mr. Ritter introduced the National Quality Council bill, signed into law by President Bush in 1992. (241)

———

 Studies show that 90% of production costs stem from design issues that may consume less than 5% of the development budget. (95, p. 48)

———

 Information technology is sure to have a profound effect on our productivity. In Japan, Toyota buyers can select any combination of features and colors they desire on Monday morning and pick up the car on Friday. Even more amazing, buyers of America's Motorola pagers can order from a variety of features in several million combinations and have the finished product shipped to them *within two hours.* (293)

———

Fallacy: We need big productivity gains, not little ones, to remain productive.

 Fact: If you do not think that little improvements can make a big difference, consider what happened when Georgia-Pacific changed to thinner saw blades that take a smaller bite out of logs. The wood that used to become sawdust on the sawmill floor can now be made into 800 railcars full of Georgia-Pacific products each year. (33, p. 78)

———

∎ It costs twice as much to make a Coca-Cola can as it does to make the drink that fills the can. (85)

Quality

Canadian owners of the Rumanian-built Dacias automobile have experienced problems such as leaky fuel tanks, gearshift knobs that fall off in the driver's hand, burned-out headlights, and batteries, starters, fan blowers, and windshield-wiper motors that failed within the first four months of ownership. When confronted with these problems, the Rumanian distributor of the Dacia in Canada said "North American owners don't really earn the right to drive cars because they aren't first-class mechanics." (323)

Since 1969, 2,200,000 copies of *How to Keep Your Volkswagen Alive* have been sold worldwide. (188).

According to a 1980 survey by J. D. Power and Associates, owners of cars from the Big Three U.S. auto companies had *three times* the problems with their cars within 90 days of purchase than did owners of Japanese cars. The U.S. manufacturers had only 25% more complaints by 1990. (94, p. 25)

The U.S. General Accounting Office (GAO) concluded that the *management systems* used by the Japanese auto assemblers operating in the United States were the *primary* source of their production efficiency and product quality. (418, p. 2)

Fallacy: The GAO surveyed corporate executives, and discovered many were creating substantial barriers to their U.S. firms being able to implement comprehensive quality management practices. The barriers were caused by falacies they believed were true, including:

∎ No change is necessary (some CEOs are not convinced they need to focus on quality because the company is doing well financially).

∎ A short-term view of profits is appropriate.

∎ There is no need to change their culture (such as giving greater authority to employees).

∎ Comprehensive quality management is a fad.

∎ Raising quality means increasing cost (e.g., higher expenditures on training).

Fact: To counteract these fallacies the GAO notes the following facts:

Quality management improves profitability. In 1989, The Conference Board sent a questionnaire to senior executives of large U.S. corporations. Of the 149 firms answering the questionnaire, 62 (42%) had attempted to measure how improving quality affects productivity. Of those companies that were trying to measure quality's impact on their profits, about 75% said that profits had increased noticeably because of *lower cost* and/or an *increased market* share resulting from these higher-quality products. (418, pp. 76–77)

 Likewise, the GAO noted that PIMS Associates, Inc., correlated data collected on more than 1,000 businesses and concluded that those selling high-quality products and services were generally more profitable. They also found that both return on investment and market share rose with quality. (418, pp. 6–7)

 As far back as 1983, a report on the Japanese Deming prize winners published by the Japanese Union of Scientists and Engineers also noted that the financial performance of winners was above the average of their industries. (418, p. 8)

∎ The U.S. GAO examined companies that were improving their quality. Those companies used several measures to assess the impact of quality management: timeliness of delivery, reliability, order-processing time, production errors, product lead time, inventory turnover, quality cost, and cost savings. What did they find? As seen in the accompanying figure, every measure improved when the company focused on quality. Reliability improved 11.5%. Most of the companies improved their performance in all dimensions.

Not all companies surveyed measured the cost of quality. Those that did not cited problems of defining cost factors and the administrative burden of collecting such data. All companies that did measure it reported that these costs dropped an average of 9% annually. These savings included the cost of quality failures or defects (lost profits, rework, and scrap) or the cost of trying to avoid them (inspection, testing, and training). (213, p. 23)

Improvement from Focusing on Quality

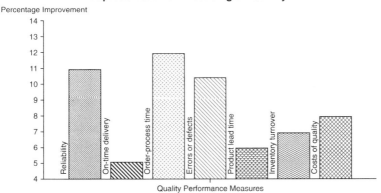

Source: U.S.General Accounting Office.

Where should a manufacturer start when trying to improve quality and performance? Many experts believe the ideal place to begin is by reducing cycle time, which is the total time required to complete a particular business process, such as producing a product. Steven Hronec of consulting firm Arthur Andersen and Company estimates that most companies that have not tried to reduce their cycle time could reduce it by 80–90%. (453, p. 71)

It costs money to have good quality. An analysis by Phillip Crosby Associates, Inc., a U.S. quality consultant and writer, shows that, for instance, British banks waste more than 50% of their entire operating cost because of error-prone procedures that result in lost documents. An average 30% of sales is wasted in manufacturing and service operations in France and 40% in Italy because of poor quality. (204, p. 27)

Fallacy: The cost of poor-quality products and services to most companies is less than 10% of sales.

Fact: Studies show this cost of quality is more likely to be in the *20–40% range* with the industry average being close to 25%. (355, p. 61)

Fallacy: Upper management has a good idea of the cost and benefits of good or poor quality.

Fact: The American Society for Quality Control commissioned the Gallup organization in 1986 and 1987 to conduct telephone opinion surveys of senior business executives. *One in five had no idea* what producing poor-quality products cost their company. (418, p. 7)

A 1989 survey by the Gallup organization discovered that top executives were aware of the role of quality management in meeting foreign competition, but senior executives regarded the greatest challenge as coming from other U.S. companies. (418, p. 7)

Fallacy: Today, everybody is into the "quality movement."

Fact: No. Only *10%* of American service companies today have any kind of quality program, reports Gunneson Group International, a quality consulting company in Landing, New Jersey. But the good news is that by the year 2000, 70% of those with more than 500 employees will have formal quality initiatives. (202, p. 100)

———

Fallacy: American consumers are primarily interested in the lowest price, as opposed to quality.

Fact: According to a Yankelovich Clancy Shulman poll taken in the spring of 1990, Americans rank quality's components in this order: reliability, durability, easy maintenance, ease of use, a known or trusted brand name, and finally, a *low price.* (200, p. 44)

———

Fallacy: Make a quality product and they will come.

Fact: It takes more than quality; it takes understanding your customers' needs. A major U.S. manufacturer of appliances managed to gain entry into the Japanese market. Its outsized stoves and mammoth refrigerators won the prompt admiration of Japanese buyers. But the tight living quarters of the average Japanese home did not allow kitchen space for the standard American models. Worse still, the narrow width of Japanese doorways often meant it denied entrance into the kitchen. Reports are that in some Japanese homes, these bulky American refrigerators are situated in unused parts of the house—admired as an art object or status symbol! (299, p. 19)

———

Fallacy: Quality problems are caused by employees' poor work habits and poor attitudes.

Fact: W. Edwards Deming and J. M. Juran, world-renowned quality experts, estimate that 85% of quality problems are management's doing, such as strapping workers with inferior machines. (203, p. 16)

Fallacy: The Japanese have taken over the U.S. market for stereo equipment.

Fact: True for the *mass* market. But at the high end of the market, U.S. firms reign supreme. There is a $400 million world market of customers who pay up to $100,000 for a home music reproduction system. These well-heeled customers with golden ears buy *American* stereo gear, such as a $5,600 disk player from Wodia, a $2,495 preamplifier from Audio Research, a $22,000 power amplifier from Jeff Rowland, and $9,200 speakers from Thiel. (45)

Good news and bad! First the good news: 55% of Americans (compared to 48% four years ago), give high quality rankings to products made in the United States. The bad news is that the rest of the world does not agree with the Americans. Only 17% in Japan and 26% in Germany gave American products a thumbs up. Moreover, only 3% of Japanese and 21% of Germans thought American workers cared about the quality of the products they produced or the services they performed. (395)

Fallacy: You can rely on the accuracy of information in computerized databases.

Fact: Often you cannot. A 1991 survey of information executives in 50 large firms revealed that half of them thought that information in their companies' databases was less than 95% accurate. Practically all were skeptical of using the databases in individual departments for making important decisions. (68) Quality in the future will rely more on information. That information must be accurate!

Fallacy: Japanese auto manufacturing plants based in the United States buy parts from Japanese suppliers because they cannot get the quality they need from U.S. parts suppliers.

Fact: Certainly not true in every case. For example, Manchester Stamping Corporation of Manchester, Michigan, shipped 540,000 parts to Honda of America in 1989. *Only seven were bad.* (453, p. 72)

∎ Someone once said "Once is not enough," but *one* may be enough, at least in the area of quality. In 1980 with 5,000 suppliers and a shipment defect rate of 8%, Xerox moved to "single sourcing." This was the forerunner of the popular "vendor certification" so popular in the 1990s. As a result, Xerox's cost of materials dropped by 50% and its overhead for its material management area dropped by two-thirds. An additional bonus was the fact that defects fell from 10,000–25,000 per million to an impressive *350* per million. (3)

Fallacy: There is a limit to how good you can make a product. Standards can be set too high.

Fact: Some companies have exceptional quality standards.

Motorola, Inc., in the United States is experimenting with an almost unheard-of goal of 60 defects or fewer for every *billion* components it makes. (203, p. 8)

Fallacy: One-hundred percent good stuff is an impossible goal to reach in business.

Fact: Zero defects is a reality in many cases. L. L. Bean filled 500,000 catalog orders for the firm's outdoor gear without an error during the spring of 1992. During 1991 the firm claims that it never fell below 99.9% accuracy in filling customer orders. (453, p. 72)

Research and Development

Fallacy: Japanese businesses spend more on research and development (R&D) than do American businesses.

Fact: The United States spends almost twice as much on research and development than Japan and Germany *combined*. But that is not the whole story. (214, p. 15)

Fallacy: U.S. R&D expenditures are comparable to those of foreign competitors.

Fact: During the 1970s, the United States spent considerably *less* on civilian R&D than any of its major industrial competitors (strange, considering the previous fact, but true nevertheless). U.S. *civilian* R&D spending ran at about 1.5% of gross national product, compared with an average of 2% for other major industrial nations. Significantly, in the 1950s and 1960s, this country spent more, not less, on civilian R&D than did its overseas competitors. But U.S. total R&D spending fell from 7.1% of GNP in 1976 to 2.8% in 1986. While the proportion is similar to that of Japan and Germany, the structure of U.S. research and development is different from that of its chief competitors. Fifty-five percent of the United States' R&D is devoted to the military. Since military R&D is neither process nor consumer oriented, this R&D spending does little to help U.S. firms compete. (327, p. 53)

Fallacy: We are investing a greater share of our GNP in R&D than Japan in an effort to compete better against them.

Fact: Japan's investment as a percentage of its GNP is nearly twice that of America's. Also, the competitive targets of U.S. R&D and capital investments changed during the past decade. In 1980, 9.3% of federal spending went into investments in plant and equipment, nondefense R&D, and education. This fell to 6.5% by 1990. During the 1980s, most capital spending by manufacturers covered fast-depreciating items like trucks and computers, instead of new factories and tools. (17, p. 16)

Fallacy: Now that the cold war is over, a larger percentage of public R&D money in the United States has been converted to nondefense purposes.

Fact: Defense R&D still makes up 31% of U.S. government R&D expenditures, down no more than a couple of percentage points from the 1960 level. (78, p. 25)

Japan has *70,000 more* scientists and engineers working on R&D in its labs than the United States has. (339, p. 60)

Fallacy: Japan has more scientists and engineers than does the United States.

Fact: The United States' 5.5 million scientists and engineers are double the number in Japan—and they have won more Nobel prizes than did scientists from all other nations combined. (214, p. 15) Pretty impressive, right? Well, it gets better. Consider the following.

The U.S. pool of scientific talent from 1985 to 1988 included 790,000 scientists and engineers engaged in R&D on a full-time basis. This compares to an estimated 381,000 for Japan and 330,000 for the United Kingdom, Germany, and France *combined.* (436, p. 3)

Fallacy: U.S. companies are innovators; Japanese firms are copiers.

Fact: Not according to one view of this issue. Toshiba of Japan leads in a new measure of companies' technological strength. The measure, developed by Francis Narin, is based on how many times a company's U.S. patents are cited relative to those of all other companies. The resulting index is multiplied by the number of a company's patents to find the firm's technological strength. For 1991, the top-ranked U.S. company is Eastman Kodak. It is ranked fifth overall, however, trailing four Japanese firms: Toshiba, Hitachi, Canon, and Mitsubishi Electric. (159, p. 68)

═══

Fallacy: American and Japanese companies follow the same approach in their R&D.

Fact: They follow opposite approaches. American firms invest about 80% of their R&D money in new product development and 20% in improving existing products. Japanese firms reverse this, investing 80% to improve existing products and 20% to develop new products. (77) This helps Japan get lower production costs and better production methods. We try to automate to eliminate labor costs, or we seek cheap, offshore labor. (17, p. 22) We often send the critical work of building primary component parts for the new products we create to the Japanese because they are so good at that. An example is Apple Computer giving Sony the specifications to build the PowerBook notebook computers that Apple designed because Sony has miniaturization skills that Apple does not possess. This is a good example of a strategic alliance that helped Apple get a new, innovative product to market faster. But Sony never before built computers. It can now, can't it?

═══

Over half of Hewlett-Packard's sales come from products that are *less than three years old.* At any time, more than 500 product development projects are in progress in the company. (102, p. 92)

In the past few years Japan has been spending more than *twice* as much as the United States on private investment. (377, p. 52)

Fallacy: R&D must come from America's large corporations, because small businesses cannot afford it.

Fact: Firms with fewer than 500 employees doubled their share of America's corporate R&D during the 1980s, raising it from 6% to 12%. (1, p. 95)

It takes the Japanese 40 months to get a new car to market while it takes Americans 60 months, but it's not just the Japanese we have to worry about. The United Kingdom is able to get a pharmaceutical to market in *2-1/2* months, one-half the time it takes American firms. (248, p. 5)

Thirty-three percent versus 4%. McKinsey and Company, a management consulting firm, notes that high-tech products that come to market six months late but on budget will earn 33% less profit over five years. In contrast, coming out on time and 50% over budget cuts profits only 4%. Whoever said speed kills was not talking about new product development. (235, p. 54)

Fallacy: It is best to keep a new technology secret, develop it within one's own company, and then try to market it alone.

Fact: Sony learned otherwise in the videotape market. Why did the VHS format beat out Sony's Beta format in the marketplace? Because JVC quickly shared its VHS format with other companies, making that format the more popular one for videocassettes. (12, p. 56)

In 1985, the last year for which such figures are available, 85.4% of American scientists and engineers with Ph.D.s were male and 88.7% of them were Caucasian, although both shares are declining. (215, p. 72)

Flypaper? *Scientific American* held a paper airplane contest in 1967. Enthusiasts turned in 12,000 designs! (114, p. 139)

■ Who says we are not creative? In 1987, Americans wrote over a third of the world's scientific articles. Japanese wrote 7% of them, while West Germans authored 6%. (20, p. 130)

Fallacy: The United States publishes more technical and scientific papers than does any other nation.

Fact: The United States is the runner-up, and you will never guess which country is number one. Believe it or not, *Israel* publishes 10 times more technical and scientific papers than does the United States. Do you suppose the fact that its people have the world's best math skills and that it has more scientists per capita has anything to do with this? (58, p. 253)

In the spring of 1992, production began on a new type of lightweight, bright and clear monitor. Eventually, they will appear in television sets that consumers will hang on their living room walls or fit in their briefcases. A variety of companies will produce them, that is, a variety of Japanese companies. No American company produces them, though the technology was invented in the United States, pioneered by David Browdy of Westinghouse. Westinghouse invested in his R&D work, but the money dried up when he needed to develop the *manufacturing* process required for commercial production. (439, pp. 19–27)

In basic research it's not always clear where the research will take you. Unexpected benefits or detours have produced some of the major advances of our time. These include high-temperature superconductor lasers, biotechnology, fiber optic communication, personal computer spell-checkers, and biological pest control. (414, pp. 1–2)

A recent example illustrates how unexpected results can come from basic exploration or research. In 1979, researchers using the National Science Foundation's supported submersible *Alvin* found vents releasing very hot water along a mountain range under the Pacific Ocean. They saw sulfur-blackened water shooting out of tall rock "chimneys" at superhot temperatures. As part of their basic research, the team saw and sampled deposits of metal ores (zinc, iron, copper, calcium, and magnesium).

The ores were what researchers had expected to find. What came as a great *surprise* was the discovery of a whole new life system associated with these vents—species that use sulfur as energy, the way other animals use sunlight and oxygen. (414, p. 2) Only time will tell if the basic research produces economic and practical applications, but much of today's current basic research is already doing just that. (414, pp. 1–2)

———

Ninety percent of R&D in the United States is performed by the manufacturing sector. (386)

———

The bulk of R&D for multinational corporations is done in their homeland. For example, a 1983 survey of 23 German multinationals showed 83% of their R&D personnel was concentrated in their home country although only 65% of their employment was in their home country. DuPont does 90% of its R&D at home, although 65% of its assets and 76% of its total employment are outside its home country. (378, p. 119)

 Researchers involved in basic research at Chicago's Institute of Gas Technology produced a strain of bacteria that extracts sulfur dioxide (a major component of acid rain) from coal without degrading the coal. Up to 90% of inorganic sulfur can be removed biochemically or by other means.

Organic sulfur is another story; it remains chemically bound within coal's molecular structure. It is more difficult to remove, but there is also good news here. Bacteria discovered by environmental microbiologist John Kilbane can remove up to 91% of the organic sulfur. The hope is to remove all sulfur from coal before it is burned. (414, pp. 4–5)

Fallacy: Thomas Edison invented the incandescent electric light bulb.

Fact: Two Canadians beat him to it six years before Edison announced the discovery. In at least one respect the Canadians' light bulb was more advanced than Edison's because it used nitrogen in the bulb as is done today.

Edison bought the rights to the two Canadians' patent while he was conducting his own experiments. The *Toronto Star* notes that a Russian applied for a patent at the same time as the two Canadians, Woodward and Evans, did and that Edison's was given because he also produced the base, equipment, and power to make it practical. Almost 20 years before Edison, an English physicist, Sir Joseph Wilson Swan, produced an electric light, but it was inefficient. (437)

Safety in the Workplace

The chances of a 35-year-old man becoming disabled from accident or illness are 19 times as high as his chances of dying. The same chances are 37 times as high for a 35-year-old female. (145)

The ultimate occupational hazard? From 1983 to mid-1992, 30 U.S. Postal Service workers were murdered by their fellow employees. (148)

Fallacy: Worker safety is a high priority of the U.S. government.

Fact: There are 800 Occupational Safety and Health Administration (OSHA) inspectors for almost 3.6 million employers with about 55 million workers. That works out to 1 inspector for every *4,500 employers,* or 1 inspector for every 68,750 employees. (426, p. 2)

Fallacy: The threats of OSHA fines for violation of safety laws is a strong deterrent.

Fact: In 1988, the average penalty for a *serious* violation was $261.00. (426, p. 2)

Fallacy: Safety and health standards protect us from workplace chemical and health hazards.

Fact: It is estimated that the number of new chemical products introduced into the workplace ranges from 1,000 to 3,000 *each year.* OSHA regulations cover only about 630 substances, most of which are accounted for by a single air contaminants standard. This standard specifies permissible exposure levels but does not include exposure monitoring, medical surveillance, or removal. Fewer than *30* substance hazards to health are regulated by more comprehensive standards. (426, p. 21)

48 Hours
An employer has 48 hours to report a fatal accident to OSHA, even though it is generally recognized that getting to an accident scene quickly enhances an investigation. (426, p. 37)

Service Management

Fallacy: In the United States, the shift toward a service economy is a fairly recent occurrence.

Fact: The shift toward services has been under way for at least 150 years, and the growth in service employment as a percentage of total employment is right on the trend set in the 1870–1930 period. (330)

Fallacy: Businesses are benefiting from the huge investment in computers during the 1980s.

 Fact: America's service companies invested an average of $9,000 per employee in high-tech productivity tools during the 1980s. But the output per worker crept up only 0.2% per year. The manufacturing sector spends less than half as much on computer technology as does the service sector, but it has achieved greater productivity gains in recent years. (29, pp. 46–47)

Fallacy: Ninety-nine percent service is exceptional service!

Fact: Why isn't it good enough for American business to be 99% accurate? Consider these examples of what that level of performance means:

▪ At least 20,000 wrong drug prescriptions each year

183

- More than 15,000 newborn babies accidentally dropped by doctors/nurses each year

- Unsafe drinking water almost one hour each month.

- No electricity, water, or heat for 8.6 hours each year

- No telephone service or television transmission for nearly 10 minutes each week

- Two short or long landings at O'Hare airport each day (also in New York, Los Angeles, Atlanta, etc.)

- Nearly 500 incorrect surgical operations per week (30, p. 27)

Fallacy: Our service sector, like our manufacturing sector, continues to make productivity strides.

Fact: The number of service jobs in America has exceeded the number of manufacturing jobs since 1955. Output per hour in the United States' service sector has risen less than half a percent annually since 1979. (31, p. 54)

Fallacy: Japanese service businesses are more advanced than their American counterparts.

Fact: Quite the opposite is true. American service firms are generally bigger, more automated, and less sheltered from competition. (2, p. 65)

Fallacy: Since service jobs are low-wage jobs, they will always pay much less than manufacturing jobs.

Fact: This common belief rests on the assumption that service jobs are low-technology jobs and cannot be made otherwise. This need not be the case. A country can choose to excel in service sectors that generate high-wage jobs, or it can develop technologies for low-wage sectors that will boost wages there. Because Germany and Japan have better used these strategies so far, service wages in those countries range from 85% to 93% of manufacturing wages, while in the United States, service wages are only two-thirds of manufacturing wages. (100, p. 50)

The service sector, as opposed to manufacturing, now employs more than 70% of the U.S. labor force. Knowledge-based services grew by one-third in the 10-year period 1975–1985 and knowledge-intensive manufacturing grew by 40%. (240, p. 228)

═══════

Fallacy: U.S. jobs are rapidly shifting from the manufacturing sector to the service sector.

Fact: Not yet, according to the Bureau of Labor Statistics, which estimates that in 1995 74.3% of U.S. jobs will be in the service sector, up only 1.5% from 1985. (23, p. 50)

═══════

Service workers have more education, on the average, than do manufacturing employees; at equivalent levels of education, they make less. As of 1989, average hourly pay in U.S. manufacturing was $9.70, excluding benefits, compared with $8.10 in the service sector (20% lower). Service workers earn less in part because more of them are women, and they tend to be younger. (240, p. 234)

═══════

70% Seventy percent of workers in the fast-food industry are *20 years old or less.* (248, p. 38)

═══════

Fallacy: You can't export services.

Fact: Service accounts for about one quarter of U.S. exports, according to the Office of Technology Assessment (OTA). (240, p. 5)

Small Business

Fallacy: Most U.S. employers are *big businesses.*

Fact: Most of them are small firms. Based on statistics gathered from Dun & Bradstreet, more than 90% of American businesses employ 50 or fewer employees. What's more, over half of those businesses employed from 1 to 4 employees. (226)

In fact, 99% of all businesses in the United States can be considered "small business" under the definition of the government (nonfarm, nongovernment business with fewer than 500 employees). (227)

■ Risky business? The Small Business Administration estimates that up to 75% of new businesses fall by the wayside during the first few years of operation. (227)

■ The fact just noted has been a rule of thumb for many years, but that may not be the whole story. According to the National Federation of Independent Business, 77% of start-ups since the mid-1980s survived beyond their third year (of course, there is a difference between surviving and making a profit). (34, p. 84)

About half of small businesses with fewer than 10 employees do not offer health insurance coverage to their employees with cost being the primary reason cited for not doing so. (421, p. 1)

150% Health care costs for small business firms with fewer than 25 employees increased at one and-one-half times the rate experienced by the nation's largest firms. (421, p. 2)

50% Likewise, about half of the working insured, or 3.9 million workers, are employed by firms with fewer than 25 employees. (423, p. 5)

Fallacy: It's the big employers that add most of the jobs in the United States.

Fact: The facts say otherwise. About 46% of the value added in U.S.-manufactured products comes from 355,000 manufacturers with fewer than 500 employees. Between 1980 and 1986, manufacturing firms with fewer than 100 employees added 326,000 jobs, while those employing 500 or more shed 1.8 million jobs. (113, pp. 88, 90)

The OTA estimates that the Japanese government gives about 20 times more financial aid to that country's small businesses than the U.S. government gives to U.S. small businesses. (113, p. 96)

Fallacy: Small business is not very important to manufacturing in Japan.

Fact: Small and midsized businesses play an even greater role in Japan's manufacturing than similar-sized American firms play in the United States. The Japanese firms account for about 75% of manufacturing jobs in Japan, while the American firms account for 35% of production employment in the United States. (113, p. 94)

Small businesses tend to hire more Hispanic employees, but they hire fewer African-American employees than larger employers. Five percent of employees working for firms of 500 or more are Hispanic. In companies employing fewer than 100, 6.5% are Hispanic. Large employers have 11.1% African-American employees. In smaller companies the figure is closer to 8.5%. (248, p. 21)

Society and Business

Fallacy: Americans measure success by how much money they make!

Fact: It's way down on the list, according to the Roper Organization. The largest percentage (about 45%) of Americans define success in terms of "Being a good spouse and parent"; 35% said being true to yourself was how they defined success. Being true to God had about the same percentage. About 20% defined success as having friends who respect you. About 18% said being of use to society was a measure of success, and another 18% said being knowledgeable was a measure of success. Fifteen percent said being wealthy was how they defined success, while having power and influence and being prominent rated even lower. (281)

═══

 A mere 3% of Americans earn their living farming, timbering, fishing, and mining. Many of them are part-time farmers who earn most of their income doing nonfarm work. (100, p. 40)

═══

Fallacy: American high school students may not be faring well against their peers in other countries on algebra, calculus, and geometry tests, but they are competent to lead productive lives in today's industrial world.

Fact: No doubt many are. But consider that of the 2.5 million young people who graduated in 1988, it is estimated that 25% of them cannot

188

▮ Read at the eighth-grade level.

▮ Summarize a newspaper article.

▮ Write an intelligent job application letter.

▮ Solve common, real-life arithmetic problems.

▮ Interpret a bus schedule. (39, p. 8)

 People can read, but can they think? Oregon, which leads the nation in SAT scores, gave a literacy test to its adult population. Only 35% of those surveyed could determine the right amount of medicine to give a child by using a chart that specified dosages according to the child's age and weight. (259, p. 144)

 In 1988, Japan's functional literacy rate was better than 95%. In America, it's 80%. (264, p. 101)

Fallacy: America is one of the most literate and well-educated countries in the world.

Fact: Twenty-three million U.S. adults are functionally illiterate. The U.S. literacy rate is only 49th out of 158 countries in the United Nations. (326)

Fallacy: There are 23 million adult Americans who can't read.

Fact: There is not a single measure of illiteracy. Ninety-six percent of young adults read well enough to find information in a newspaper article. But when they find that newspaper article, can they make any sense out of its contents? Twenty-seven million Americans (11% of our total population) sign their name with an X, cannot fill out a simple form, and can read English no better than they can read Japanese. (326)

Fifty percent of current factory employees need to upgrade their skills in reading, writing, and basic math. This statement comes from Bill Wiggehorn, president of Motorola University and corporate vice president of Training and Education at Motorola, Inc. (392, p. 6)

 Who needs it, anyway? Recent studies funded by the National Science Foundation (NSF) show that only 5% of American adults know basic scientific facts, and that this percentage changed little between 1957 and 1987. (414, p. 41)

∎ Among the 12 largest democracies, the United States ranks 11th in voter turnout for presidential elections. (188)

 Although it is hard to believe, according to the American Association for the Advancement of Science, only half of all Americans know that the earth moves around the sun, and only half of that group knows how long it takes. (295)

 According to a report to the NSF, as of 1990 approximately two-thirds of the U.S. adult population could not read or comprehend a newspaper or magazine story about a current scientific or technological controversy. (338, pp. 7–8)

As evidence of this, the researchers surveyed the population about their scientific and technical knowledge. According to that study,

 ∎ 55% believed that humans lived at the same time as dinosaurs (half-jokingly referred to as the Fred Flintstone factor).

∎ 15% did not know the oxygen we breathe comes from plants.

In the same 1990 study, fewer than 1% of Americans who did not complete high school met the NSF's criteria for scientific literacy; 32% of those earning a graduate or professional degree were seen as scientifically literate. Overall, the NSF judged 7% of Americans scientifically literate (scientific literacy involved a minimal understanding of the processes of science, minimal understanding of scientific terms and concepts, and a minimal understanding of the impact of science on society). (338, pp. 13–14)

One quarter of all American children are born out of wedlock, and 42% of them will live in a single-parent family before they reach their 18th birthday. (264, p. 103)

Fallacy: While there are more illegitimate births now in the United States than during previous years, these births are still the exception rather than the rule.

Fact: Not much of an exception these days. As noted, 26%, or over one quarter, of *all* American babies were born to single women in 1988. These include 63% of all African-American babies, 34% of Hispanic ones, and 18% of all white babies (8).

Fallacy: Most out-of-wedlock births are among teenagers.

Fact: It is true that between 1980 and 1989 unmarried teenagers delivering babies increased by 40%, but the percentage of women in their late twenties giving birth out of wedlock increased 84%. In

1989 there were *593,500* out-of-wedlock births for women in their twenties compared to *348,000* out-of-wedlock births for teens. Interestingly, one reason given for the trend is the strong decline in hourly wages, which means that fewer men earn enough to support a family. Since both women and men work, marriage is no longer an economic necessity. (345)

———

Fallacy: With more job sharing and part-time work today in the United States, parents spend more time with their children than they did 25 years ago.

 Fact: No. Parents spend 40% less time with their children than in 1965. (6)

———

 Socioeconomic status is the best predictor of a baby's economic prospects. Most single mothers are poor. The chance of children being poor rose from 16.4% to 19.6% during the 1980s, while the chances of senior citizens being poor fell from 15.2% to 11.4%. (8)

———

 Nearly half of today's children will live in a single-parent family at some point during their childhood. About one-third will experience the divorce of their biological parents, and one-fourth will live with a stepparent, according to the National Center for Health Statistics. (284)

———

▪ Divorce is the most common reason people give for going on welfare. (188)

———

Fallacy: Welfare costs are a tremendous burden on society and probably costs more per recipient than any other government program.

Fact: In 1991, welfare benefits per recipient were $1,620, but in that same year, the U.S. prison system spent $20,296 per prisoner. (188)

One-fourth of all children in the United States will be on welfare sometime in their lives. (264, p. 102)

Fallacy: Most children of alcoholics become alcoholics themselves.

Fact: *Eighty-five* percent of children of alcoholics *do not* become alcoholics. (343)

During your lifetime there is a 50–50 chance that you will be involved in a car accident with an alcohol-impaired driver. (416)

You can pay me now or pay me later! According to the House Select Committee on Children, Youth and Families, every dollar invested in prenatal care for poor women saves $3.38. But what else can you get for that dollar?

■ Every dollar in childhood immunization saves $10.00 in later medical cost.

■ Every dollar in preschool education saves $4.75 in special education, welfare, and prison cost.

∎ Every dollar in remedial education saves $6.00 in the cost of repeating a grade. (267, p. 123)

Building too many big houses? Since 1990, federal spending on prison construction has exceeded federal spending on public housing in the United States by a *4-to-3 ratio.* For 1993, former President Bush proposed no spending on federal housing. (86)

∎ An average of 39 shopping carts are stolen each hour in the United States. (89) Now you know why some supermarkets build retaining fences with narrow openings in front of their stores or charge a refundable quarter to use a cart.

∎ One of the latest crime waves in the United States gives new meaning to the term "slimeball." Thieves are stealing used cooking grease from behind Detroit and Houston restaurants. The thieves sell their gooey grab for cash to recyclers, who refine it to be used in cosmetics, paint, plastic, and animal feed. Grease thieves cost one small company that restaurants pay to haul away grease $250,000 a year. One Houston lard lifter made $60,000 one year from his slick operation. (146)

New York's finest—there's quite a few of them. The New York City Police Department (NYPD) is twice the size of the nation's second largest police force in Chicago. The NYPD has 26,756 uniformed and 9,483 non-uniformed personnel. It has over 2,000 cars, 625 scooters, 83 motorcycles, 10 boats, 5 helicopters, 107 horses, 26 dogs, and 4 robots. Ninety-four percent of its $1.6 billion budget in 1990 paid for salaries and personnel services. (103, p. 111)

Technology

Fallacy: Japan will win the coming market in high-definition television (HDTV) as it has won other electronic markets.

Fact: The United States will offer a superior technology to Japan's in the potentially very profitable HDTV market. Japan's HDTV products will be based on older analog technology, while the American version will use newer and sharper digital signal technology. (128, p. A1)

———

Ceramics and ceramic composites are altering business. Promising new uses include automobile engines, gas turbines, and bearings. Use of ceramic in any of these applications could improve U.S. competitiveness, reduce the need for critical metals, improve energy efficiency, and reduce pollution. (436, p. 39)

———

One of the most impressive technological advances is in the area of "micromachines." Engineers have already made progress on

▮ A motor smaller than a snowflake, driving equally tiny rotor blades. It would be designed to move through human arteries, zapping plaque that clogs them.

195

▪ Robots no bigger than gnats, but like Pac-Man, able to scarf up toxic chemicals from polluted water. They could also look for cracks inside huge machinery or filter minute particles of precious minerals.

Both these advances are far from science fiction due to spin-off technology from microscopically detailed etching of integrated circuits, creating breakthroughs in building microsized machines (a micron is one-thousandth of a millimeter, or about 0.000039 inch). It's technology that can produce motors the width of a human hair with teeth the size of blood cells and springs, cranks, and tongs so small they might accidentally be inhaled.

 Already Cornell University researchers (414, p. 21) have developed a pair of electrically driven tweezers 2 microns long that can grasp an *individual* blood cell. At the University of Wisconsin-Madison, the National Science Foundation supported engineers who have built the world's smallest high-precision metal machines that someday could power miniature robots or microknives used in delicate surgical operations. At Bell Labs in New Jersey, researchers Kaigham Gabriel and William Trimmer have made turbines and working gears 125 microns in diameter. Gear teeth are 15 microns wide—less than one-fifth the thickness of a human hair. Richard Muller and colleagues at UC-Berkeley have built an entire working electric motor that is the width of a human hair. (414, pp. 22–23)

———

Fallacy: When it comes to technology, America should "close ranks" and not share it with foreigners under any conditions!

Fact: Over 60% of research published in engineering and technology originates outside the United States. A published report by the National Academy of Engineering titled "Strengthening U.S. Engineering Through International Cooperation" notes that protectionism is discouraged "Since technology inevitably diffuses." The report calls for better promotion of international cooperation in engineering research. (304)

Japan accounted for over two-thirds of 536 foreign investments in U.S. high-technology companies between 1988 and 1991. (339, p. 62)

Fallacy: Japanese electronic firms capitalize on U.S. technology breakthroughs, but do not share their technology with American firms.

Fact: This is beginning to change. For example, Toshiba has exchanged important semiconductor technology with Motorola at a jointly owned plant in northern Japan. Also, Toshiba started a flat-panel display joint venture with IBM in 1991. This Japanese electronics giant also works with General Electric and Time Warner. (62)

Fallacy: Early on, IBM saw the great potential of the personal computer market.

Fact: IBM initially forecast a *total* market for 200,000 personal computers. By the end of 1992, almost *twice* that number sold *each week!* (136)

 It is costing more these days to develop base technologies. The dynamic random access memory (DRAM) chips that are at the heart of today's personal computers are a good example of these rising costs. In 1985, the 256K DRAM, state of the art then, cost about $100 million to develop and another $100 million for a production facility. The next generation of 1-megabyte DRAMs cost about $250 million to develop plus a $200 million capital investment to produce. It is estimated that the next generation of 4-megabyte DRAMs will cost almost $500 million to develop and nearly half a billion dollars for a manufacturing facility. (106, p. 155) The level of R&D and capital investment needed to compete has more than doubled with each successive generation of semiconductors since the mid-1970s. (107, p. 57)

Get to market on time! How much cumulative profit can a printer manufacturer lose if its laser printer hits the market six months behind schedule? If we assume that the market is growing 20% a year, that prices are falling 12% a year, and that the printer will have a five-year product cycle, the company can lose one-third of the profits it might have had. (106, p. 157)

Just how fast is computer technology advancing? Consider these facts:

∎ Every year microprocessor performance improves 50%.

∎ Data storage capacity rises almost 100%.

∎ Every three years, memory density improves 400%, and its price falls. (96, p. 5)

Fallacy: Computer technology is advancing as fast as it probably ever will.

Fact: It will advance even faster in the future. A major reason: Intel Corporation plans to introduce new chip families every two years, a pace much faster than now. Intel is trying to stay ahead of competitors who are cloning their chips and underselling Intel. (87, p. 87)

Japan has 10 times the number of robots as the United States has on its assembly lines. (339, p. 60)

U.S. firms are currently experiencing an estimated *50% to 75%* failure rate when implementing advanced manufacturing technologies. (356, p. 64)

U.S. companies turn out 25 different products on each piece of equipment versus *240* products for their Japanese competitors. According to Harvard Business School professor Robert Hayes, this is due to not making better use of new technology like flexible manufacturing systems (FMS) that can turn out a wide range of products on the same line, shifting quickly from one model to the next. (269)

Fallacy: Now that the quality of many U.S. products compares well to that of competing Japanese products, manufacturing competition between the two nations will be less intense.

Fact: Not! The competition is shifting from *quality* to another factor: *flexibility.* While we have talked about flexible manufacturing systems during the past few years, Japanese manufacturers have acted. Aided by a competitive domestic capital equipment market that offers Japanese firms prices 30% below those in the United States, the Japanese installed 390,000 industrial robots to the United States' 45,000 by 1992. Japan's Okuma Corporation makes the world's broadest line of machine tool products, and they sell 14 FMSs in Japan for every one that they sell to the United States. This means that the Japanese lead may be widening.

The importance of FMSs is that U.S. manufacturers emphasize customer service and reliability slightly more than do their Japanese competitors. While staying close to us on these factors, the Japanese place much more emphasis on flexibility through product variety, innovation, and better technology. These are the factors the Japanese will bring to the future competitive battleground. (167, pp. 63–74)

CEO and the bag of chips! Each of Frito-Lay's 10,000 salespeople carry hand-held computers that zap data nightly to computers in their home office. The significance of this? CEO Wayne Calloway of their parent company, PepsiCo, noted that as late as 1980 they could not tell you how many Doritos they were selling west of the Mississippi. With their new system, not only can they tell you how Doritos are selling in California, but how they are doing in Orange County, in the town of Irvin, in the local Von's store, in a special promotion, at the end of aisle four on Thursday. (234, p. 68)

Big Brother is watching you! One estimate says that information about the average American is processed by a computer database up to 40 times a day. (429, p. 80)

In the future, tiny radio transmitters embedded in credit cards may reveal the identities of shoppers as they walk in the store or the department. (324, p. 57)

A sophisticated computer system called New Image lets prospective customers visually try on a variety of new hairdos (curls, red hair, etc.). Landscapers are using similar systems to provide instant visualizations of trees and shrubs around one's house. (324, p. 63)

Talk about a labor-saving device. PROFS, which is just one part of a computer network called VNET, saved IBM from buying 7.5 million envelopes. IBM would need an estimated *40,000 additional employees* if it did not have PROFS. (99, p. 103)

An Austin-based management consulting firm predicts that 60 million households will contain fax machines by the year 2000. The heart of this new market is people who work at home—about 25 million people work at least part time in their homes. As fax machines and their use become cheaper, they could provide a real threat to the U.S. Post Office. (272)

The price-performance ratio of digital technologies improves 25–50% a year and is expected to do so until the end of the century. This will drive an increase in inexpensive personal digital products, including personal computers, pagers, and fax machines. It should also help speed the decline of centralized systems, such as mainframe computers. (107, p. 57)

Really cool music? Sony Corporation has developed a semiconductor laser that emits a blue light that can focus on a much smaller dot than can the red light now used in compact disc (CD) players. If Sony can develop a marketable version of this, it would be possible to pack 3.5 hours of digitized music on a 5-inch CD. The problem? In its present form, the semiconductor only works at temperatures around minus 295 degrees Fahrenheit. That's just about right for music buffs who live on the moon! (156)

Fallacy: Electronic books on read-only compact disks (CD-ROMs) have not caught on with the public.

Fact: It seems that way because of the newness of this technology and its low sales so far. The fact is that sales of CD-ROM disks that store huge amounts of text, graphics, and sounds are up from 100,000 in 1988 to an estimated 2 million ($600 million in worldwide sales) in 1992. The future for electronic books also looks bright: The Bureau of Electronic Publishing forecasts sales to grow 80% a year during much of the 1990s. While the electronic novel may be years away, electronic books are especially attractive to people who need to find information quickly from among huge text and databases, such as encyclopedias. (166)

Computer on! A voice typewriter is a reality. The Dragon Dictate Voice Typewriter consists of software and a speech recognition circuit board for personal computers. Users speak into a microphone and see text appear on a video at a rate of 35 words a minute. It can recognize 30,000 words and adapt to individual speakers. (438)

 The Defense Advanced Research Projects Agency (DARPA) is involved in some of America's most advanced research. It notes that the first *gigaops* (100 billion operations per second) computing systems are beginning to emerge and by the middle of the decade DARPA expects to have systems in the *teraflops* (1 trillion floating point operations per second). (257, p. 7)

∎ DARPA is exploiting a breakthrough in the chemistry of conducting polymers for production of revolutionary solid state batteries with exceptional high density and 100 times the shelf life of nickel-cadmium batteries. They are safe and will not explode even if heated, punctured, or short-circuited. (257, p. 7)

Fallacy: Most of today's technological change is occurring in manufacturing, as opposed to services.

Fact: Technical change in today's service sector often is faster than in manufacturing. (20, pp. 110–111)

 The Persian Gulf War was only two-thirds as devastating in Kuwait as the allied forces intended. That is because one-third of the ordinance they dropped there has yet to explode. (90)

What is in the future for computers? According to the NSF, some of the possibilities include

∎ "Teraflop" supercomputers that perform more than a trillion mathematical operations per second. Such equipment helps improve the operations of robots in manufacturing and simulates human responses to new drugs (without having to test the drugs on people or animals).

∎ "Gigabit" networks whose fiber optic cables replace copper telephone lines. Such networks allow information exchange at the rate of 50,000 single-spaced typed pages a *second.* That is 1,000 times faster than nearly all the data networks now in use. (414, p. 28)

For the 1985–86 academic year, 22% of the estimated 317,000 foreign students in U.S. colleges studied engineering, but only 3% of the 30,000 U.S. college students studying abroad were enrolled in engineering or computer science. Foreigners are sharing, but it appears we are not. (304)

Fallacy: Low prices are the key to Wal-Mart's retailing success.

Fact: Low prices help, but so does a companywide communication system that helps Wal-Mart get information from all its stores within 90 minutes after they close each day. This helps them change the mix of products they ship to the stores at least once a day, which better meets customer's needs. Wal-Mart replenishes the stock in its stores an average of twice a week, compared to once every two weeks for Sears and K-Mart. (150, p. 3)

Training

Fallacy: American workers learn continuously on the job.

Fact: Only 55% of Americans are prepared for their jobs, and only 35% receive any upgrading once they are on the job. There are significant variations, with 92% of nontechnical professionals, 75% of general managers, 57% of clerical, 43% of sales, and a low of 18% of laborers receiving job preparation training. (248, p. 24)

Fallacy: American workers are well-trained.

Fact: Only one-third of American employees get *any* formal training after they go to work. Informal training (e.g., coaching) is three to six times more common than formal training. In the United States, most training and development is focused on white-collar and technical employees rather than on production and service personnel. (248, p. 5)

Fallacy: Well, at least we spend about the same on training as our overseas competition.

Fact: One study by the Olsten Corporation showed that a majority, or about 65%, of companies spend no more than $500 a year to train each hourly employee. What's more, only 46% spend more than $1,000 a year for each salaried employee. (26)

Fallacy: A study prepared by the Bureau of Labor Statistics for the U.S. Congress entitled *"Workforce 2000: Is Corporate America Prepared?"* revealed that two-thirds of all American manufacturing firms *spend less than $2,000 annually on training new employees,* and many domestic organizations spend nothing at all. What's more, only 5% of American manufacturing firms spend more than $5,000 annually on classroom or on-the-job training for new employees. (361)

Fact: We may believe it, but few act as if this is the case. In the United States, we know we will have fewer young people entering the work force during the 1990s, so it is imperative that we make our current work force as productive as possible. But we budget less for training than do our overseas competitors, and 68% of what we do spend goes for more schooling for college grads—managers, technicians, professionals, and supervisors. Our biggest problem and greatest need is to train craftspeople and production workers. (17, p. 23)

Knowing what to do and doing it are two different things. *Eighty percent* of human resource executives say their need for workers with solid literacy skills rose during the last five years. But less than 25% say their companies are spending money to improve writing skills—even though 65% said these skills needed boosting. This is reported by the Center for Workplace Issues, which surveyed 455 human resource executives. (255)

Is this asking so much? Motorola is a world-class company and winner of the United States' first quality award. Their managers demand three capabilities of their manufacturing workers:

∎ Seventh-grade communication and computation skills. This will increase soon to eighth- and ninth-grade levels.

∎ Ability to do basic problem solving individually and in small groups.

∎ Acceptance of a workweek long enough to ship perfect product to the customer. (108, p. 71)

━━━

Forty-nine and one-half million workers, or 42% of the work force, will need additional training, according to information released by the American Society for Training and Development (ASTD). They will need the training to keep up with new demands of their jobs but *will not get that training* if present practices continue. There will be 16 million needing skills and technical training, 5.5 million needing executive, management or supervisory training, 11 million needing customer service training, and an amazing 17 million needing basic skills training. All this training does not include the 37 million who need entry level or "qualifying" training. (294)

━━━

Fallacy: Japanese auto-assembly workers must get twice as much training as their U.S. counterparts.

Fact: Would you believe *six* times as much? The Japanese often get 300 hours of training during their first six months on the job. New U.S. workers get 50 hours of training. (117, p. 52) Japanese automakers based in the United States give their seasoned production workers an average of 53 hours of training per year. U.S. automakers train their experienced workers 29 hours per year. (121)

━━━

According to the Bureau of Labor Statistics, as late as 1988, roughly 1 million workers on the job three years or more have been displaced annually. About 30% of them lack the basic skills of reading, writing, and arithmetic. (265)

━━━

Training involves wearing different colored hats, writing down dreams, or "mindmapping" (drawing a diagram using squares and circles to capture a flow of thought). Well, a survey of 2,600 companies by The Conference Board found that 32% offered this *creativity training* in 1991 (up from 22% in 1989). Such "off-the-wall" training has received a lot of criticism, but the board said Frito-Lay's creativity enhancement program produced cost reductions of $100 million over a four-year period during the 1980s. (305)

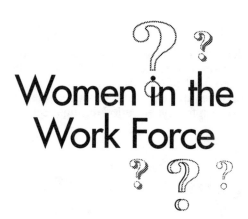

Women in the Work Force

Fallacy: Being female in a foreign country is a distinct disadvantage.

Fact: In a study of females who had completed foreign assignments, almost half (42%) said being female served more as an advantage than a disadvantage in their foreign managerial positions. Sixteen percent found being female to have both positive and negative effects, 22% saw it as irrelevant or neutral, and 20% found that being female was a negative. Thus it usually is not a disadvantage to be female in a foreign culture. (325, p. 16)

Fallacy: Women do not want to work overseas.

Fact: In a recent study of Canadian and American firms that sent managers abroad, only 3% were female. On the other hand, in a study of 1,129 females graduating with MBAs from seven management schools in the United States, about 84% said they would like an international assignment at some point in their careers. (325, p. 13)

 According to *American Demographics* magazine, women are most likely to be discriminated against, have greater difficulty in getting high-visibility assignments that lead to more responsibility, and experience more sexual harassment when they choose careers as military officers, investment bankers, farmers, flight attendants, book editors, day care workers, retail buyers, and large-firm attorneys. They are least likely to be discriminated against and subject to sexual harassment and more likely to receive higher-visibility jobs in engineering, personnel management, health care, hospitality, finance, teaching, and veterinary medicine. (300)

 It's not being swept under the rug anymore. One year after Anita Hill's testimony in the fall of 1991, the number of sexual harassment complaints filed with the Equal Employment Opportunity Commission was up 45%. (188)

Fallacy: There will be an equal number of men and women entering the work force.

Fact: Women will account for about three in five new workers by the year 2000. (334)

Fallacy: More American men than women are taking on second jobs.

Fact: Since 1970, the number of American men working more than one job rose 1%, while the number of American women doing so rose 390%. (46)

45% Women make up 45% of the U.S. work force. The Department of Labor projects that 84% of women of child-bearing age will be working by the year 2000. (97, p. 5)

 More Americans work today than ever before: 66.3% of the population was employed in 1991. It was not quite 60% in 1950. Most of this surge is due to women. In 1950 about one-third of women worked; in 1991 that figure had risen to 57%. (357, p. 51)

50% By the year 2000, women will make up half the labor force, but not the top half. In a study by *Fortune* in 1990, of the 4,012 people listed as the highest-paid officers and directors of the 1,000 largest U.S. industrial and service companies, only 19 women, or less than 1%, were included. (353, p. 40)

Glass ceiling training? A survey by Catalyst, a New York–based research firm, showed that 7% of participants at eight prestigious executive training programs (Harvard, Columbia, etc.) were women. The reason is that most of the participants were supposed to be senior-level managers. Since only 5% of these positions are occupied by women, the low percentage could be expected. The study also revealed that human resource professionals believed women had comparable ability to men, 48% believed women had less career commitment, and 43% thought women had less initiative and took fewer risks. (380)

Fallacy: Men are usually more committed to their jobs than women.

Fact: According to one study, it depends on with which sex they are working. One finds the strongest commitment when males work with other males. Males' commitment falls as the percentage of females they work with rises. Women's commitment stays constant regardless of the number of males with whom they work. (54)

Fallacy: Very few women run companies, it is mostly businessmen!

Fact: Women-owned, nonfarm sole proprietorships more than *doubled* over the decade from 1.9 million in 1977 to 4.4 million in 1987. In 1977, the number of nonfarm sole proprietorships owned by men exceeded the number owned by women by a margin of 3.3 to 1. But women's share of businesses owned rose from 22.6% in 1977 to 30.7% in 1987. (229, p. xvii)

Many of the women who decided to go to work to earn a second income for their family did so by starting a business. As more women do this, lenders will become more used to granting loans to women. Also, more women in business will foster networks (good ol' girls?), and they will be able to help each other more with business problems.

Fallacy: Practicing law is men's work.

Fact: Women made up 20% of lawyers in 1991, compared to 5% in 1970. (41)

Fallacy: The vast majority of graduates from university business schools are males.

Fact: Increasing numbers of women now seek business degrees. They now earn 55% of undergraduate accounting degrees and 35% of MBA degrees. (79, p. 108)

 Hewitt Associates, a benefits and compensation consulting firm in Chicago, found that of the 259 major employers in the area, 56% offered some sort of child care aid, 56% allowed flexible scheduling, and 42% granted unpaid parental leave. (353, p. 54)

■ A female's place is at work; sort of. In manufacturing, two-thirds are men, while 45% of employees in the trade are women. Women also constitute 60% of employees in "other services" (data processing, recreation, hotels, health, etc.) (240, p. 234)

Fallacy: About the same number of men and women use personal computers.

Fact: Twice as many women as men use personal computers, according to a survey commissioned by mouse manufacturer Logitech. The poll did find that women avoid making adjustments to their computers and that they read fewer computer magazines. (134)

Sixty-nine percent of all school-aged kids have mothers in the work force, up from 39% in 1970. Women with children under age 6 are the fastest-growing segment of the work force. (266, p. 112)

Work Force Attitudes and Demographics

Fallacy: Employees are only interested in getting a paycheck and going home.

Fact: Money is a factor, but not the most important one, according to a survey on employees' attitudes toward their jobs and quality improvement programs conducted for the American Society for Quality Control by the Gallup organization. Data were presented to the National Quality Forum VI in 1990. In response to the question, "How companies can improve job performance," the survey showed that 33% of employees felt management should let them do more to put their ideas into action. They saw this as the most important way to improve job performance. True, 27% said paying them more was most important, but an impressive 19% said the most important way to improve job performance was to give them more recognition, and 17% said the most important way was to listen to their ideas for improvement. Thus three of the four motivational factors were not money. Even the most frequently chosen response did not involve money. (236, p. 177)

———

Fallacy: Management is watching out for their "people."

Fact: Not if you believe what the "people" think. A poll of 1,115 working people conducted by Diagnostic Research discovered cynicism about management and others' motives. To the question, "Will management take advantage of you if you let them?" 72% agreed or were in doubt. When they were asked to respond

213

to the statement "A lot of people in my company do enough to just get by," 73% agreed or were not certain.

Other responses show a similar cynicism toward management. Sixty-eight percent thought management makes an unfair salary, 59% felt management was more interested in profits than people, 66% often doubted the truth of what management tells them, and 42% felt it does not pay to work extra hard in their company. Do you think that in this time of mergers, acquisitions, and downsizing that there might be a credibility problem in the American workplace? (444)

Fallacy: American production employees don't care about work or being productive.

Fact: In a study by Rath and Strong, Inc., 22,000 American manufacturing workers were surveyed to determine their views about the work climate, their supervisors, and themselves. Over two-thirds of all hourly employees stated that work is not assessed or redesigned regularly enough to keep employees as productive as possible. Fifty-seven percent see a great need to improve the work climate, with the greatest needs in the areas of performance feedback, career development, and conflict resolution. (296)

 Our work force is becoming more educated. In 1979, 16% of jobholders in America had completed at least four years of college. By 1988, 21% of them had reached that level of education. (229, p. xv)

 Many Japanese businesses have only 4 job classifications; U.S. autoworkers have over 50. (336, p. 7)

Fallacy: The high cost of U.S. labor is a main reason we are not competitive with the Japanese.

Fact: Average hourly wage costs in 1988 were $13.90 in the United States and $13.14 in Japan. American top executive salaries are much higher than those of Japanese CEOs. Compensation of middle managers compares this way: $85,649 in Japan, $56,505 in the United States. (24, p. 9)

 Which of the world's employees have the strongest loyalty to their company? A study by *Fortune* magazine used a score of 100 to represent the strongest employee identification with company values. The United States finished third. Japanese workers scored 85, while West Germans scored 64. The U.S. score of 56 was only slightly higher than the United Kingdom's 48 score. (358, p. 61) If this were a test score, we would probably be hoping someone would grade on the "curve."

Fallacy: American businesses take care of their workers.

Fact: Less than a third of U.S. businesses offered their laid-off workers any job placement or counseling to facilitate reemployment. (424, p. 11)

---

30 or Less The U.S. General Accounting Office (GAO) reports that more than 80% of the United States' larger businesses that closed or had a large layoff give their employees fewer than 30 days' advance notice. (424, p. 35)

Studies have found that providing assistance to reduce anxiety and help workers cope with problems is an essential element of successful dislocated worker projects. However, in 1987, less than 25% of dislocated worker project participants received *any* form of support services. (424, p. 53)

 It is estimated that between 850,000 and 1 million Americans will be employed by Japanese companies in the United States by the turn of the century. (335, p. 87)

Seventy-five percent of the future U.S. work force is already in place, according to The Conference Board. The lesson for business seems to be that you had better make do with what you have. (332, p. 57)

 One-fourth of all 15-year-olds and one-half of all 16-to 17-year-olds worked some time during the year 1988. That included over 4 million children. (369, p. 2)

Fallacy: Exploitation of child labor long ago ceased to be a problem in the United States.

Fact: Not according to the National Child Labor Committee (NCLC). According to the NCLC, 250,000 children work illegally on U.S. farms, many of them migrants. Almost every city with many poor immigrants has sweatshops. There also are many violations in small, fragmented industries such as small manufacturers, subcontractors, apparel manufacturers, and restaurants. (155, p. 87)

Fallacy: Low-income and minority children are the ones most likely to be employed.

Fact: High-income and white children are more likely to be employed. In 1988, 32% of children whose families earned less than $20,000 were employed. This compared with 54% of the children of high-income families (incomes above $60,000). (369, p. 2)

 There are fewer teenagers than people over 65, and by 1995 the number of 17- to 22-year-olds will have dropped by 3 million. (332)

Late in 1989, McDonald's franchisees in Boston went all the way to Ireland seeking workers. (231, p. 314)

∎ Profit-sharing plans are used in over 400,000 companies across North America. (231, p. 315)

50% **Fallacy:** Alternate work arrangements (e.g., work at home) are more prevalent at small companies, such as those in service industries.

Fact: About 50% of large companies surveyed by the U.S. GAO said they were considering, had in place, or planned to use alternate work schedules. About half of the large employers (minimum of 25,000 employees) also were considering job sharing as a viable alternative to the traditional single-person, 40-hour-a-week job. (362, pp. 11–12)

1 in 4 As of 1988, an estimated 32 million workers did not fit the traditional model of full-time permanent employment. By 1988, part-time, temporary, contract, and other nontraditional workers made up 25% of the work force. In 1989, one out of every five workers in the United States was a part-timer. (364, pp. 2–17)

If you add the self-employed, the part-time, temporary (voluntary and involuntary), plus illegal immigrants, and people who work at home or in the underground economy, the total reaches 25–30% of U.S. employment. (240, p. 246)

Fallacy: People who work part time do it because they can't find full-time work.

Fact: In 1989, 77% of part-time workers voluntarily chose this employment status, according to the Bureau of Labor Statistics. They paid the price for this freedom because part-timers make 38% less per hour than do full-time workers (even after controlling for education, gender, and age). (364, p. 5)

 Involuntary part-time work accounts for 5–6% of total U.S. employment—a small percentage, but one that represented 5.5 million people at the beginning of 1987. (240, p. 246)

 Making ends meet! About 20–25% of those who work part time hold two or more jobs by choice or by necessity (roughly 5 million Americans report holding multiple jobs). The largest percentages are in public works (7.6% clustered in teaching and state and local government) and agriculture (6.1%) (240, p. 246)

Fallacy: Temporary employment means that someone will be employed "temporarily" and for a short time.

Fact: According to the U.S. GAO, there is no standard definition of the time period beyond which a worker can no longer be considered temporary. For example, Pacific Telesis Group, a major employer in the San Francisco Bay area, uses nonpermanent employees for periods ranging from a day up to three years. Temporary workers can work either full-time or part-time schedules. On an average day in 1989, over 1 million people, about 1% of the work force, worked as temporary help. (364, pp. 18–19)

Fallacy: Most people who become self-employed begin with a small amount of capital.

Fact: Not according to U.S. and British government data. Studies show that wealthy people are the ones most likely to become self-employed. Wage workers who enter self-employment tend to be white, older, and married, and to have relatively high levels of education. (37)

———

 "Why do they have to get all the good parking spaces?" A survey conducted for the Bureau of National Affairs showed good news and bad. The good news was that 52% of U.S. workers think it would be fair to have their own work schedules or even job duties changed to accommodate a new coworker who has a disability, while 16% said it would be unfair and would protest. Four out of 10 don't know anyone with a disability, but perhaps that is because most do not understand what is and is not a disability. Half of those surveyed didn't think cancer or AIDS was a disability, but they are, according to the Americans' Disability Act (ADA). On the other hand, a majority thought illiteracy was a disability, but it is not, according to ADA. (381)

———

Fallacy: Doing a good job at work is the key to success.

Fact: Not unless it includes "politicking." A survey of 428 managers by Gandy and Murray showed that 90% of them said workplace politics is common in most organizations, and most surprisingly, 89% of them said successful executives must be good politicians. They also noted that 76% believed that the higher one progresses up the organization, the more political things become. Over half (55%) said that politics were detrimental to efficiency. (375)

———

Fallacy: It is the blue-collar employees who are expendable and most at risk of unemployment.

Fact: Equal pain: In early 1992, roughly the same number of white-collar and blue-collar workers were unemployed in the United States. (90)

Work Force

Fallacy: As businesses downsize and organizations become flatter, there will be little need for supervisors.

Fact: During this time of team management, there is a shortage of supervisors, and it is expected to get worse. A report from the Hudson Institute and Tower Perrin, a research center and management consulting firm, respectively, notes that the following job categories will experience labor shortages: secretarial/clerical, skilled crafts, technical, professional, administrative, and *supervisory/management.* (301)

---

2 + 2 = ? The National Academy of Sciences reported that 20% to 30% of dislocated workers lack basic skills. (424, p. 22)

 Employers largely agree that entry-level workers should read at least at an eighth-grade level, but some 20% of young Americans function *below that level.* The U.S. GAO notes that increasingly the technological content of many entry-level jobs requires 11th- or 12th-grade reading and computation skills. The GAO projects that by the time they reach age 25, about 9 million of America's 33 million youth, now aged 16 to 24, will not have skills needed to meet employer requirements for entry-level positions. These 9 million include 5.5 million dropouts and the 3.8 million high school graduates who lack high school competency. (425, p. 2)

———

Fallacy: More American employees work for Japanese firms than work for any other foreign country.

Fact: Japan is third. The United Kingdom employed 981,000 U.S. workers at the end of 1989. Canada is second with 755,000, and Japan is a distant third with 504,000. Germany is close behind Japan with 436,000. (289)

———

Fallacy: African Americans in the United States are making little economic progress.

Fact: The Los Angeles riots in May 1992 will probably reinforce this fallacy. But the facts are that the percentage of African Americans in white-collar occupations has doubled since 1966, now standing at 45%. This has lowered the poverty rate of African Americans from 42% then to 30% now. Over 11.5 million African Americans now work in managerial, professional, and technical jobs. By any measure, that is progress! (76, p. 41)

———

Fallacy: Future labor force growth in the United States will consist mainly of American males.

Fact: Not according to the Hudson Institute, whose prognosticators estimate that over the next 13 years, only 15% of the entrants to the U.S. work force will be white males. Sixty percent will be women. Most of the rest will be African Americans and immigrants. (39, p. 7) In 1987, 56% of women aged 16–68 were in the work force, as were 68% of women with children under 6 years of age. By the year 2000, those two figures will rise to 65% and 90%, respectively. (41, p. 23)

———

■ The rate of U.S. population growth continues to slow. (224)

∎ Meanwhile, the growth of the work force continues to change. (225)

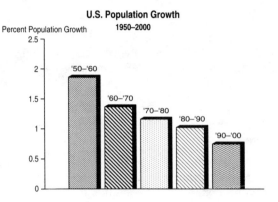

Source: Bureau of the Census.

Source: Bureau of Labor Statistics.

■ A larger proportion of the work force will consist of women during the 1990s. (225)

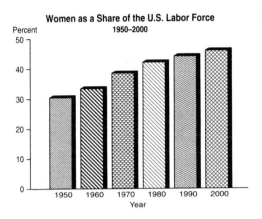

Source: U.S. Bureau of Labor Statistics.

■ There will be more minorities, and forecasters expect 57% of new job entrants to be nonwhites. This is twice their current share. Forecasters project that immigrants will make up more than 23% of the labor force by the year 2000. (225)

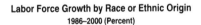

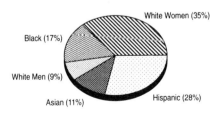

Source: Howard N. Fullerton, Jr., "Labor Force Projections: 1986 to 2000," Monthly Labor Review, Vol. 110, No. 9 (September 1987), pp. 19–29.

∎ Even the growth of the age groups will change. (224)

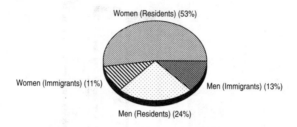

Components of Projected Labor Growth
Immigrant or Resident Status and Gender, 1986–2000

Women (Residents) (53%)

Women (Immigrants) (11%)

Men (Immigrants) (13%)

Men (Residents) (24%)

*Source: Howard N. Fullerton, Jr., "Labor Force Projections: 1986 to 2000,"
Monthly Labor Review, Vol. 110, No. 9 (September 1987), pp. 19–29.*

∎ There will be 2 million fewer workers aged 14 to 16 in the 1990s. (224)

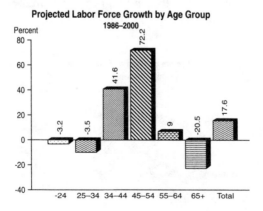

Projected Labor Force Growth by Age Group
1986–2000

Percent

-24: -3.2
25–34: -3.5
34–44: 41.6
45–54: 72.2
55–64: 9
65+: -20.5
Total: 17.6

Source: Bureau of Labor Statistics

Employment in the manufacturing industry is projected to decline by more than 800,000 through the end of this century, even though forecasters expect manufacturing output to rise 2.3% per year.

———

 Good ol' days? The sweatshops of the 1880s and 1890s make today's work pretty tame. Garment sweatshops were typically located in the worst tenement buildings, often in basements or attics, or over saloons or stables, and were frequently noxious with refuse. Working hours were unlimited, and people worked until they fell asleep from exhaustion. Quite common was a working day of 15 or 16 hours, from 5 in the morning until 9 at night. A fair average wage for a New York cloak maker was $9.00 a week. That week consisted of six working days of 14 or 15 hours each. (397)

REFERENCES

1. Reich, Robert B., *The Work of Nations: Preparing Ourselves for 21st Century Capitalism*. New York: Alfred A. Knopf, 1991.

2. Nasar, Sylvia, "America Still Reigns in Service," *Fortune*, June 5, 1989, p. 65.

3. "The Benefits of Single-Supplier Relationships," *Managing Technology Today*, Vol. 1, No. 1, May 1992, p. 5.

4. Rose, Frank, "Now Quality Means Service Too," *Fortune*, April 22, 1991, p. 100.

5. Eberstadt, N., "Population Change and National Security," *Foreign Affairs*, Vol. 70, No. 3, 1991, pp. 115–131.

6. Whitmire, R., "Crisis: Two-Parent Homes Panacea for U.S. Woes, Coalition Says," *The News-Leader* (Springfield, Missouri), June 23, 1991, p. 5B.

7. Whitmire, R., "Moving Up: Change Welfare Rules to Reward Positive Behavior, Experts Say," *The News-Leader* (Springfield, Missouri), June 23, 1991, p. 5B.

8. Will, G., "Poverty as Health Problem Needs New Medicine," *The News-Leader* (Springfield, Missouri), June 23, 1991, p. 6B.

9. Richman, L., "The Coming World Labor Shortage," *Fortune*, April 9, 1990, pp. 70–76.

10. Toy, S., J. B. Levine, M. Maremont, and I. Reichlin, "The Battle for Europe: Japan Muscles in on the West—And a Shakeout Begins," *Business Week*, June 3, 1991, pp. 44–52.

11. Magnusson, P., S. Baker, D. Beach, G. DeGeorge, and C. Symonds, "The Mexico Pact: Worth the Price?" *Business Week*, May 27, 1991, pp. 32–35.

12. Stewart, T. A., "Brainpower," *Fortune*, June 3, 1991, pp. 44–60.

13. Kanter, Rosabeth Moss, "Transcending Business Boundaries: 12,000 World Managers View Change," *Harvard Business Review*, Vol. 69, No. 3 (May–June 1991), pp. 151–164.

14. Taylor, Alex, III, "Do You Know Where Your Car Was Made?" *Fortune*, June 17, 1991, pp. 52–56.

15. Kirkpatrick, David, "Who's Winning the Computer Race," *Fortune*, June 17, 1991, pp. 58–68.

16. Sherman, Stratford P., "Japan's Influence on American Life," *Fortune*, June 17, 1991, pp. 115–124.

227

17. Stewart, T. A., "The New American Century: Where We Stand," *Fortune,* Spring–Summer 1991, pp. 12–23.

18. Koretz, G., "CEO Pay Envelopes Are Lighter North of the Border," *Business Week,* June 24, 1991, p. 26.

19. Ohmae, Kenichi, *The Borderless World.* New York: Harper-Collins, 1990.

20. Bhagwati, J. *Protectionism.* Cambridge, MA: The MIT Press, 1988.

21. Patton, John A., "No One to Blame but Themselves," *Management Review,* October 1982, p. 16.

22. Faltermeyer, Edmund, "Is `Made in the U.S.A.' Fading Away?" *Fortune,* September 24, 1990, pp. 62–73.

23. Koepp, Stephen, "Pul-eeze! Will Somebody Help Me?" *Time,* February 2, 1987, p. 50.

24. Hitt, Michael, R. E. Hoskisson, and J. S. Harrison, "Strategic Competitiveness in the 1990s: Challenges and Opportunities for U.S. Executives," *Academy of Management Executive,* Vol. 5, No. 2 (May 1991), pp. 7–22.

25. Bernstein, A., "Family Leave May Not Be That Big a Hardship for Business," *Business Week,* June 3, 1991, p. 28.

26. "Service-Oriented and Basic Skills Offered, But Quality Is Goal," *Industrial Engineering,* Vol. 24, No. 11 (November 1992), p. 16.

27. Smith, L., "A Cure for What Ails Medical Care," *Fortune,* July 1, 1991, pp. 44–49.

28. Technical Assistance Research Programs (TARP) Institute, *Consumer Complaint Handling in America: Summary of Findings and Recommendations.* Washington, D.C. White House Office of Consumer Affairs.

29. Boroughs, D. L., G. F. Black, and D. Pasternak, "Desktop Dilemma," *U.S. News & World Report,* December 24, 1990, pp. 46–48.

30. Thomas, S., "What Is Motorola's Six Sigma Product Quality?" *Proceedings,* AAPICS International Conference, October 8–12, 1990, New Orleans, Louisiana, pp. 27–31.

31. Berger, J., "Productivity: Why It's the No. 1 Underachiever," *Business Week,* April 20, 1987, pp. 54–55.

32. Dickinson, John, "The Fight to Save Natural Resources Starts on Our Own Desktop," *PC Computing,* Vol. 5, No. 12 (December 1992), p. 122.

33. Wallace, G. D., D. Foust, T. Thompson, J. Schwartz, L. Miles, and M. Pitzer, "America's Leanest and Meanest," *Business Week,* October 5, 1987, pp. 78–84.

34. Labich, Kenneth, "The New Low-Risk Entrepreneurs," *Fortune,* July 27, 1992, pp. 84–92.

35. "Not So Trivial Trivia," *Issues and Answers* (USAA Life Insurance Company), Vol. 2, No. 4 (Winter 1993), p. 5.

36. Taylor, Alex, III, "Why Toyota Keeps Getting Better and Better and Better," *Fortune,* November 19, 1990, pp. 66–79.

37. Evans, David S., The Effect of Access to Capital on Entry into Self-employment. Washington, D.C.: U.S. Small Business Administration Office of Advocates, 1991.

38. Perry, N. J., "The Workers of the Future," *Fortune,* Spring–Summer 1991, pp. 68–72.

39. Bunke, H. C., "Pax Americana," *Business Horizons* (January–February 1990), pp. 3–8.

40. Perry, Nancy J., "Here Come Richer, Riskier Pay Plans," *Fortune,* December 19, 1988, p. 51.

41. Dwyer, P. and A. Z. Cuneo, "The `Other Minorities' Demand Their Due," *Business Week,* July 8, 1991, p. 62.

42. "Harper's Index," *Harper's Magazine,* Vol. 284, No. 1706 (July 1992), p. 9.

43. Rapaport, Carla, "Getting Tough with the Japanese," *Fortune,* April 20, 1992, pp. 149–155.

44. Krause, Axel, *Inside the New Europe.* New York: Harper-Collins, 1991.

45. Smart, Tim and Neil Gross, "This Sonic Boom Is Made in America," *Business Week,* May 4, 1992, p. 140.

46. "Harper's Index," *Harper's Magazine,* Vol. 285, No. 1711 (December 1992), p. 17.

47. Schor, Juliet B., *The Overworked American: The Unexpected Decline of Leisure.* New York: Basic Books, 1991.

48. Toy, Stewart and Seth Payne, "The Yankee Invasion Has Foreign Carriers Running for Cover," *Business Week,* July 6, 1992, pp. 54–55.

49. Richman, Louis S., "America's Tough New Job Market," *Fortune,* February 24, 1992, pp. 52–61.

50. Smith, Emily T., "Growth Vs. Environment," *Business Week,* May 11, 1992, pp. 66–75.

51. Smith, Emily T., David Woodruff, and Fleur Templeton, "The Next Trick for Business: Taking a Cue from Nature," *Business Week,* May 11, 1992, pp. 74–75.

52. Koretz, Gene, "Who Really Profits from Mortgage Interest Deductions?" *Business Week,* May 11, 1992, p. 20.

53. Templeton, Fleur, ed., "The Visible Hand Making Germany a High-Tech Heavy Hitter," *Business Week,* May 11, 1992, p. 101.

54. Koretz, Gene, "Women in the Workplace: Men Are All Shook Up," *Business Week,* May 18, 1992, p. 22.

55. Koretz, Gene, "Would the Economy Gain from Spreading Inherited Wealth?" *Business Week,* May 18, 1992, p. 22.

56. Greenberger, Robert S., "North-South Split: With Cold War Over, Poorer Nations Face Neglect by the Rich," *The Wall Street Journal,* May 14, 1992, pp. A1, A7.

57. Schlesinger, Jacob M., "Short Circuit: Electronics Industry in Japan Hits Limits After Spectacular Rise," *The Wall Street Journal,* April 28, 1992, pp. A1, A10.

58. Nixon, Richard M., *Seize the Moment: America's Challenge in a One-Superpower World.* New York: Simon & Schuster, 1992.

59. Reid, T. R. and Brit Hume, "Flash Memory Ready Faster than Predicted," *The News-Leader* (Springfield, Missouri), May 26, 1992, p. D2.

60. "Air Chow Costly, If Not Tasty," *The News-Leader* (Springfield, Missouri), June 14, 1992, p. E1.

61. Sobel, Robert, "Caveat Foreigner: Japan Learns an Old Lesson," *The Wall Street Journal,* April 20, 1992, p. A10.

62. Gross, Neil, "Toshiba: Rethinking the Way It Does Business," *Business Week,* April 27, 1992, p. 55.

63. Neff, Robert, Ted Holden, Zachary Schiller, Paul Magnusson, Jonathan B. Levine, and William Glosgall, "Japan: Will It Lose Its Competitive Edge?" *Business Week,* April 20, 1992, pp. 50–54.

64. Holden, Ted and Joyce Barnathan, "The Squeeze Felt 'Round the World,'" *Business Week,* April 27, 1992, pp. 56–57.

65. Demaree, A. T., "What Now for the U.S. and Japan?" *Fortune,* February 10, 1992, pp. 80–95.

66. Labich, Kenneth, "Airbus Takes Off," *Fortune,* June 1, 1992, pp. 102–108.

67. Deutschman, Alan, "The CEO's Secret of Managing Time," *Fortune,* June 1, 1992, pp. 135–146.

68. Bulkely, William M., "Databases Are Plagued by Reign of Error," *The Wall Street Journal,* May 26, 1992, p. B6.

69. Associated Press, "Trash on Road to Nowhere," *The News-Leader* (Springfield, Missouri), July 11, 1992, p. A1.

70. Avishai, Bernard, "Israel's Future: Brainpower, High Tech And Peace," *Harvard Business Review,* Vol. 69, No. 6 (November–December 1991), pp. 50–64.

71. Drucker, Peter F., "The New Productivity Challenge," *Harvard Business Review,* Vol. 69, No. 6 (November–December 1991), pp. 69–79.

72. Drucker, Peter F., "The Emerging Theory of Manufacturing," *Harvard Business Review,* Vol. 68, No. 3 (May–June 1990), pp. 94–102.

73. Bleike, Joe and David Ernst, "The Way to Win in Cross-Border Alliances," *Harvard Business Review,* Vol. 69, No. 6 (November–December 1991), pp. 127–135.

74. Brooks, David, "Europe: Unity Debate Starts in Danish," *The Wall Street Journal,* May 29, 1992, p. A10.

75. "Premium Education," *The Wall Street Journal,* May 29, 1992, p. A10.

76. Kirkland, Richard I., Jr., "What We Can Do Now," *Fortune,* June 1, 1992, pp. 40–48.

77. "Made in America?" Public Broadcasting System Telecast, May 26, 1992.

78. Branscomb, Lewis M., "Does America Need a Technology Policy?" *Harvard Business Review,* Vol. 70, No. 2 (March–April 1992), pp. 24–31.

79. Schwartz, Felice N., "Women as a Business Imperative," *Harvard Business Review,* Vol. 70, No. 2 (March–April 1992), pp. 105–113.

80. Kunjufu, Jawanza, a contributor to the debate, "Can Equal Opportunity Be Made More Equal?" *Harvard Business Review,* Vol. 70, No. 2 (March–April 1992), pp. 138–158.

81. Miller, Krystal, "At GM, the Three R's Are the Big Three," *The Wall Street Journal,* July 3, 1992, pp. B1, B6.

82. Hammond, Joshua, a contributor to the debate, "Does the Baldridge Award Really Work?" *Harvard Business Review,* Vol. 70, No. 1 (January–February 1992), pp. 126–147.

83. Sisodia, Rajendra S., "Singapore Invests in the Nation-Corporation," *Harvard Business Review,* Vol. 70, No. 3 (May–June 1992), pp. 40–50.

84. Morita, Akio, "Partnering for Competitiveness: The Role of Japanese Business," *Harvard Business Review,* Vol. 70, No. 3 (May–June 1992), pp. 76–83.

85. "Harper's Index," *Harper's Magazine,* Vol. 283, No. 1697 (October 1991), p. 15.

86. "Harper's Index," *Harper's Magazine,* Vol. 284, No. 1703 (April 1992), p. 13.

87. Hof, Robert D., "Inside Intel: It's Moving at Double-Time to Head Off Competitors," *Business Week,* June 1, 1992, pp. 86–94.

88. "Harper's Index," *Harper's Magazine,* Vol. 281, No. 1685 (October 1990), p. 17.

89. "Harper's Index," *Harper's Magazine,* Vol. 284, No. 1701 (February 1992), p. 11.

90. "Harper's Index," *Harper's Magazine,* Vol. 284, No. 1702 (March 1992), p. 13.

91. Korr, Albert R., "Labor Letter," *The Wall Street Journal,* June 2, 1992, p. A1.

92. Capulsky, Jonathon R. and Michael J. Wolf, "Relationship Marketing: Positioning for the Future," *The Journal of Business Strategy,* Vol. 11, No. 4 (July–August 1990), pp. 16–20.

93. Batres, Roberto E., "One Market for the Americas," *The Journal of Business Strategy,* Vol. 13, No. 2 (March–April 1992), pp. 13–17.

94. DeSouza, "Designing a Customer Retention Plan," *The Journal of Business Strategy,* Vol. 13, No. 2 (March–April 1992), pp. 24–28.

95. Sisodia, Rajendra S., "Why Companies Kill Their Technologies," *The Journal of Strategic Management,* Vol. 13, No. 1 (January–February 1992), pp. 42–48.

96. Crouse, Henry J., "The Power of Partnerships," *The Journal of Business Strategy,* Vol. 12, No. 6 (November–December 1991), pp. 4–8.

97. Heenan, David O., "The Right Way to Downsize," *The Journal of Business Strategy,* Vol. 12, No. 5 (September–October 1991), pp. 4–7.

98. Koretz, Gene, "Why the Taxman Wants You to Refinance Your Home," *Business Week,* November 2, 1992, p. 22.

99. Toffler, Alvin, *Powershift.* New York: Bantam Books, 1990.

100. Thurow, Lester, *Head to Head: The Coming Economic Battle Among Japan, Europe, and America.* New York: William Morrow, 1992.

101. Murray, Alan, "The Outlook: An Alternative Agenda for the Rio Summit," *The Wall Street Journal,* June 8, 1992, p. A1.

102. House, Charles H. and Raymond Price, "The Return Map: Tracking Product Teams," *Harvard Business Review,* Vol. 69, No. 1 (January–February 1991), pp. 92–100.

103. Webber, Alan M., "Crime and Management: An Interview with New York City Police Commissioner Lee P. Brown," *Harvard Business Review,* Vol. 69, No. 3 (May–June 1991), pp. 110–126.

104. Fisher, Anne B., "The New Debate Over the Very Rich," *Fortune,* June 29, 1992 pp. 42–54.

105. Korr, Albert R., "Labor Letter," *The Wall Street Journal,* June 9, 1992, p. A1.

106. Nevins, T. Michael, Gregory L. Summe, and Bro Uttal, "Commercializing Technology: What the Best Companies Do," *Harvard Business Review,* Vol. 68, No. 3 (May–June 1990), pp. 154–163.

107. Ferguson, Charles H., "Computers and the Coming of the U.S. Keiretsu," *Harvard Business Review,* Vol. 68, No. 4 (July–August 1990), pp. 55–70.

108. Wiggenhorn, William, "Motorola U: When Training Becomes an Education," *Harvard Business Review,* Vol. 68, No. 4 (July–August 1990), pp. 71–83.

109. Jones, John P., "The Double Jeopardy of Sales Promotions," *Harvard Business Review,* Vol. 68, No. 5 (September–October 1990), pp. 145–152.

110. HBR Photo File, "The Corporate Search for Identity," *Harvard Business Review,* Vol. 68, No. 5 (September–October 1990), pp. 153–157.

111. Drucker, Peter F., excerpts from "Behind Japan's Success" (article originally published in January–February 1981 issue), *Harvard Business Review,* Vol. 68, No. 4 (July–August 1990), p. 163.

112. Halberstam, David, *The Reckoning.* New York: William Morrow, 1986.

113. Howard, Robert, "Can Small Business Help Countries Compete?" *Harvard Business Review,* Vol. 68, No. 6 (November–December 1990), pp. 88–103.

114. O'Connor, John T., "Elegant Design for Everyday Life," *Harvard Business Review,* Vol. 68, No. 1 (January–February 1990), pp. 134–139.

115. Stevenson, Douglas F., of the National Council of Insurers. Letter to the authors, May 19, 1992.

116. Hale, David D., "Global Finance and the Retreat to Managed Trade," *Harvard Business Review,* Vol. 68, No. 1 (January–February 1990), pp. 150–162.

117. Stone, Nan, "Does Business Have Any Business in Education?" *Harvard Business Review,* Vol. 69, No. 2 (March–April 1991), pp. 46–62.

118. "Reed, Paul and Otto Dobnick, "Wisconsin Central Limited—A Regional Railroad," a case presented at the annual meeting of the North American Case Research Association, November 3–5, 1992, New Orleans, Louisiana.

119. Stein, Herbert, "Deficits, Disaster, and Ross Perot," *The Wall Street Journal,* June 17, 1992, p. A16.

120. Joseph, James A., "Leadership for America's Third Century: The Imperatives of a Civil Society," *National Forum,* Vol. 71, No. 1 (Winter 1991), pp. 5–7.

121. "Harper's Index," *Harper's Magazine,* Vol. 284, No. 1705 (June 1992), p. 13.

122. Smith, Lee, "Coping with the Defense Build-Down," *Fortune,* June 29, 1992, pp. 88–93.

123. Eiben, Therese, "U.S. Exporters on a Global Roll," *Fortune,* June 29, 1992, p. 94.

124. Seligman, Daniel, "Keeping Up," *Fortune,* June 29, 1992, pp. 111–112.

125. Sookdeo, Ricardo, a portion of "What the Amazing Japanese Are Up to Now," *Fortune,* June 29, 1992, p. 13.

126. Rogers, Alison, a portion of "What the Amazing Japanese Are Up to Now," *Fortune,* June 29, 1992, p. 13.

127. Vogel, Thomas T., "Taiwan Now Is Big Buyer of Treasurys," *The Wall Street Journal,* July 13, 1992, pp. C1, C15.

128. Rose, Robert L., "Electronic Edge: How U.S. Firms Passed Japan in Race to Create Advanced Television," *The Wall Street Journal,* July 20, 1992, pp. A1, A4.

129. Smith, Keith V., "The Stock Market Doesn't Mind Democrats," *The Wall Street Journal,* July 20, 1992, p. A10.

130. Karr, Albert R., "Labor Letter," *The Wall Street Journal,* July 14, 1992, p. A1.

131. Mandel, Michael J., Christopher Farrell, Doris J. Yang, Gloria Lau, Christina Del Valle, and S. L. Walker, "The Immigrants: How They're Helping to Revitalize the U.S. Economy," *Business Week,* July 13, 1992, pp. 114–122.

132. Deutschman, Alan, "The Upbeat Generation," *Fortune,* July 13, 1992, pp. 42–54.

133. Rapaport, Carla, "'Them,'" *Fortune,* July 13, 1992, pp. 96–98.

134. Losee, Stephanie, "Surprise! A PC Gender Gap," *Fortune,* July 13, 1992, p. 14.

135. Lublin, Joann A., "Companies Use Cross-cultural Training to Help Their Employees Adjust Abroad," *The Wall Street Journal,* August 4, 1992, p. B1.

136. Stahlman, Mark, "Creative Destruction at IBM," *The Wall Street Journal,* January 6, 1993, p. A10.

137. Koutz, Gene, "More Temps Are Called—But Will a Job Rebound Follow?" *Business Week,* June 29, 1992, p. 25.

138. Ward, Sam, "USA Snapshots," *USA Today,* August 13, 1992, p. 1B.

139. Memmott, Mark, "Accord's Benefits Will Come Gradually," *USA Today,* August 13, 1992, p. 9B.

140. Farrell, Christopher, "Where Have All the Families Gone?" *Business Week,* June 29, 1992, pp. 90–91.

141. Kerwin, Kathleen et al., "Detroit's Big Chance: Can It Regain Business and Respect It Lost in the Past 20 Years?" *Business Week,* June 29, 1992, pp. 82–90.

142. Segal, Troy et al., "When Johnny's Whole Family Can't Read," *Business Week,* July 20, 1992, pp. 68–70.

143. O'Reilly, Brian, "The Job Drought," *Fortune,* August 24, 1992, pp. 62–74.

144. Crystal, Graef S., *In Search of Excess.* New York: W. W. Norton, 1991.

145. USAA Life Insurance Company, "The Myths and the Facts About Disability." San Antonio, Texas: The Author, 1991.

146. Depke, Deidre A., ed., "Is Hair from the Barber's Floor Next," from the column, "In Business This Week," *Business Week,* August 24, 1992, p. 39.

147. "Toll-Free Trend Turns 25: Technology Gives Americans a 1-800 World," *The News-Leader* (Springfield, Missouri), August 23, 1992, p. 3D.

148. "Harper's Index," *Harper's Magazine,* Vol. 284, No. 1707 (August 1992), p. 13.

149. Cox, Meg, "Rhythm and Blues: Rock Is Slowly Fading as Tastes in Music Go Off in Many Directions," *The Wall Street Journal,* August 26, 1992, pp. A1, A8.

150. Ghemawat, Pankaj, *Commitment: The Dynamic of Strategy.* New York: The Free Press, 1991.

151. Fukuyama, Francis, *The End of History and the Last Man.* New York: The Free Press, 1992.

152. Verity, John W., Neil Gross, and Gary McWilliams, "The Japanese Juggernaut That Isn't," *Business Week,* August 31, 1992, pp. 64–66.

236 ■ References

153. Koretz, Gene, "Downsizing Can Push Up Workers' Comp Claims," *Business Week*, August 31, 1992, p. 18.

154. Farnham, Alan, "How They Give Their Money Away," *Fortune*, September 7, 1992, pp. 92–96.

155. Deutschman, Alan, "Why Kids Should Learn About Work," *Fortune*, August 10, 1992, pp. 86–89.

156. "Cool Development: Sony's Blue Laser," in Harris Collingwood, ed., "In Business This Week," *Business Week*, August 3, 1992, p. 32.

157. Coolingwood, Harris, ed., "In Business This Week," *Business Week*, August 3, 1992, p. 32.

158. Miller, Karen L., "Now, Japan Is Admitting It: Work Kills Executives," *Business Week*, August 3, 1992, p. 35.

159. Buderi, Robert, John Carey, Neil Gross, and Karen Lowry, "Global Innovation: Who's in the Lead?" *Business Week*, August 3, 1992, pp. 68–69.

160. Woodruff, David and Zachary Schiller, "Smart Step for a Wobbly Giant," *Business Week*, December 7, 1992, p. 38.

161. "Harper's Index," *Harper's Magazine*, Vol. 285, No. 1708 (September 1992), p. 13.

162. Reich, Robert B., "Education Reform: Don't Count On Business," *Harper's Magazine*, Vol. 285, No. 1708 (September 1992), pp. 26–28.

163. Barnard, Jeff, "Japanese Bombed Oregon in 1942," *The News-Leader* (Springfield, Missouri), September 6, 1992, p. 14A.

164. Phillips, Kevin P., "U.S. Industrial Policy: Inevitable and Ineffective," *Harvard Business Review*, Vol. 70, No. 4 (July–August 1992), pp. 104–112.

165. Henzler, Herbert A., "The New Era of Eurocapitalism," *Harvard Business Review*, Vol. 70, No. 4 (July–August 1992), pp. 57–68.

166. Schwartz, Evan I., "Scrolled Any Good Books Lately?" *Business Week*, September 7, 1992, p. 61.

167. Stewart, Thomas A., "Brace for Japan's Hot New Strategy," *Fortune*, September 21, 1992, pp. 62–74.

168. Brandt, Richard, "Chipping Away at Japan," *Business Week*, December 7, 1992, p. 120.

169. Collingwood, Harris, ed., "In Business This Week," *Business Week*, September 7, 1992, p. 38.

170. Maremont, Mark and Robert Neff, "The Hottest Thing Since the Flashbulb," *Business Week*, September 7, 1992, p. 72.

171. Therrien, Lois, "To Thwart a Thief: The Latest in Car Protection," *Business Week*, September 7, 1992, p. 98.

172. Segal, Troy, Christina Del Valle, David Greising, Rena Miller, Julia Flynn, and Jane Prendergast, "Saving Our Schools," *Business Week*, September 14, 1992, pp. 70–78.

173. National Public Radio News, September 3, 1992.

174. Toy, Stewart, John Templeman, Richard A. Melcher, John Rossant, and Stanley Reed, "Europe's Shakeout: The Race to Restructure Is Getting Frantic," *Business Week*, September 14, 1992, pp. 44–51.

175. Schwartz, Evan I., "Prodigy Installs a New Program," *Business Week*, September 14, 1992, pp. 96–100.

176. Stipp, David, "The Gender Gap," *The Wall Street Journal*, September 11, 1992, p. B8.

177. Sherman, Stratford, "Are Strategic Alliances Working?" *Fortune*, September 21, 1992, pp. 77–78.

178. "Golf Aces Tennis," *Fortune*, September 21, 1992, p. 13.

179. "Now Hear This," *Fortune*, September 21, 1992, p. 16.

180. Kleinman, Ira J., "Focus on Criteria for Credibility," *Broker World*, Vol. 12, No. 1 (January 1992), pp. 46, 74.

181. Hall, Lynn W., "A New Idea: Social Security Income Protection," *Broker World*, Vol. 12, No. 5 (May 1992), pp. 16–20.

182. Dawson, Robert W., "Long-Term Care Insurance: Refinements Improve Product Design," *Broker World*, Vol. 12, No. 5 (May 1992), pp. 46–56.

183. Hewitt, Tommy, "Payroll Deduction Prospecting: It's in the Numbers," *Broker World*, Vol. 12, No. 8 (August 1992), pp. 12–18.

184. Thau, Claude, "Exploring the `New-Collar' Market," *Broker World*, Vol. 12, No. 8 (August 1992), pp. 46–50.

185. Tayloe, Jack, "Alcohol Markers in Blood Analysis Past and Present," *Broker World*, Vol. 11, No. 11 (November 1991), pp. 44–50.

186. Johnson, Kerry, "What Do Your Clients Really Want?" *Broker World*, Vol. 11, No. 12 (December 1991), pp. 100–103.

187. Boyco, Gregory A., "Finding Great DI Products and Prospects," *Broker World*, Vol. 11, No. 6 (June 1991), pp. 90–94, 168, 174.

188. "Harper's Index," *Harper's Magazine*, Vol. 285, No. 1709 (October 1992), p. 11.

189. Tanouye, Elyse, "Body Temperature of 98.2 Degrees Found to Be Normal," *The Wall Street Journal*, September 23, 1992, p. B4.

190. Coontz, Stephanie, "A Nation of Welfare Families," *Harper's Magazine,* Vol. 285, No. 1709 (October 1992), pp. 13–16.

191. Lammers, Teri, Leslie Brokaw, et al., "Hands On: A Manager's Notebook," *Inc.,* Vol. 12, No. 9 (September 1990), pp. 130–132.

192. Grego, Susan and Michael P. Cronin, "On-the-Cheap Market Research," *Inc.,* Vol. 14, No. 6 (June 1992), p. 108.

193. Robert, Michael, "The Do's and Don'ts of Strategic Alliances," *The Journal of Business Strategy,* Vol. 13, No. 2 (March–April 1992), pp. 50–53.

194. Casey, Eugene J., Jr., "A Plan for Environmental Packaging," *The Journal of Business Strategy,* Vol. 13, No. 4 (July–August 1992), pp. 18–20.

195. "Women Buying Almost Half of New Cars Today," in "Ozarks Marketplace," *The News-Leader* (Springfield, Missouri), October 12–18, 1992, p. 12.

196. Rice, Faye, "Next Steps for the Environment," *Fortune,* October 19, 1992, pp. 98–100.

197. Richman, Louis S., "Bringing Reason to Regulation," *Fortune,* October 19, 1992, pp. 94–96.

198. Stewart, Thomas A., "U.S. Productivity: First but Fading," *Fortune,* October 19, 1992, pp. 54–57.

199. O'Reilly, Brian, "How to Keep Exports on a Roll," *Fortune,* October 19, 1992, pp. 68–72.

200. Rice, Faye, "How to Deal with Tougher Customers," *Fortune,* December 3, 1990, pp. 39–48.

201. Mather, Hal, "Don't Just Satisfy, Delight Your Customers," *APICS— The Performance Advantage* (August 1991), p. 22.

202. O'Neal, Michael, "Beyond May I Help You," in *The Quality Imperative,* published by *Business Week,* October 25, 1991, p. 100.

203. Port, Otis, "Questing for the Best," in *The Quality Imperative,* published by *Business Week,* October 25, 1991, pp. 8–16.

204. Levine, Jonathan B., "It's an Old World in More Ways than One," in *The Quality Imperative,* published by *Business Week,* October 25, 1991, pp. 26–28.

205. Hammonds, Keith H., "Where Did They Go Wrong?" in *The Quality Imperative,* published by *Business Week,* October 25, 1991, p. 38.

206. Peterson, Tom, Kevin Kelly, Joseph Weber, and Neil Gross. "Top Products for Less than Top Dollar," in *The Quality Imperative,* published by *Business Week,* October 25, 1991, p. 66.

207. Woodruff, David, "Miles Traveled, Miles to Go," in *The Quality Imperative,* published by *Business Week,* October 25, 1991, p. 70.

208. Rose, Frank, "Now Quality Means Service Too," *Fortune,* April 22, 1991, pp. 97–108.

209. U.S. Office of Consumer Affairs, *"Increasing Customer Satisfaction,"* bulletin of the U.S. Office of Consumer Affairs (Washington, D.C.), undated, pp. 1–14.

210. Technical Assistance Research Programs (TARP) Institute, "Industry-Specific Research," unpublished. Washington, D.C.: White House Office of Consumer Affairs, 1980–1985.

211. Technical Assistance Research Programs (TARP) Institute, *Consumer Complaint Handling in America: An Update Study, Executive Summary.* Washington, D.C.: U.S. Office of Consumer Affairs, April 1, 1986.

212. Technical Assistance Research Programs (TARP) Institute, *Consumer Complaint Handling in America: An Update Study, Part II.* Washington, D.C.: U.S. Office of Consumer Affairs, March 31, 1986.

213. U.S. General Accounting Office, *Management Practices: U.S. Companies Improve Performance Through Quality Efforts.* Washington, D.C.: The Author, May 2, 1991, pp. 19–35.

214. Port, Otis, "Back to Basics," in *Innovation in America,* special issue published by *Business Week,* 1989, pp. 14–18.

215. Hall, Alan, "People Scientific Talent—Both Homegrown and Imported," in *Innovation in America,* special issue published by *Business Week,* 1989, pp. 72.(??)

216. U.S. Department of Labor, *Weekly Newspaper Service* (Washington, D.C.), December 9, 1991, p. 3.

217. U.S. Department of Labor, *Weekly Newspaper Service* (Washington, D.C.), December 2, 1991.

218. U.S. Department of Labor, *Weekly Newspaper Service* (Washington, D.C.), November 4, 1991.

219. U.S. Department of Labor, *Weekly Newspaper Service* (Washington, D.C.), October 28, 1991.

220. U.S. Department of Labor, *Weekly Newspaper Service* (Washington, D.C.), October 21, 1991.

221. U.S. Department of Labor, *Weekly Newspaper Service* (Washington, D.C.), September 9, 1991.

222. U.S. Department of Labor, *Weekly Newspaper Service* (Washington, D.C.), October 7, 1991.

223. U.S. Department of Labor, *Weekly Newspaper Service* (Washington, D.C.), October 14, 1991.

224. Office of Advocacy, Office of Economic Research, *Trends in Small Business Toward the Year 2000: Demographic, Workplace, Marketplace.* Washington, D.C.: July 11, 1991.

225. *Small Business Administration, 1990 U.S.* Small Business Administration Annual Report, Vol. 1. Washington, D.C.: The Author, 1990, pp. 54–55.

226. Dun & Bradstreet, *The Challenges of Managing a Small Business.* New York: The Author, 1989, p. 1.

227. National Association for the Self–Employed, *"The Small Business Resource Guide,"* Business Administration pamphlet (Harst, Texas), p. 4.

228. Braddock Communications, *The World Is Your Market: An Export Guide for Small Business.* Washington, D.C.: The Author, 1990, pp. 5–6.

229. *The State of Small Business: A Report of the President Transmitted to Congress.* U.S. Small Business Administration. Washington, D.C.: U.S. Government Printing Office, 1990.

230. Rice, Gaye, "Champions of Communication," *Fortune,* June 3, 1991, p. 116.

231. Day, Marie, "Employee Involvement and Gainsharing," International Industrial Engineers' Conference Proceedings, May 20–23, San Francisco, California, pp. 314–315.

232. Henkoff, Ronald, "Cost Cutting: How to Do It Right," *Fortune,* April 9, 1990, p. 40.

233. Farnham, Alan, "The Trust Gap," *Fortune,* December 4, 1989, pp. 56–62.

234. Sellers, Patricia, "Pepsi Keeps On Going After No. 1," *Fortune,* March 11, 1991, p. 68.

235. Dumaine, Brian, "How Managers Can Succeed Through Speed, *Fortune,* "February 13, 1989, pp. 54–56.

236. Voss, Charles E., "Applied Techniques for Higher Employee Involvement," *Manufacturing Principles and Practices Seminar,* April 22–24, 1991, Orlando, Florida, p. 177.

237. Farrell, Christopher and Michael J. Mandel, "Industrial Policy," *Business Week,* April 6, 1992, p. 74.

238. Wayne Calloway, PepsiCo Year End Address to Employees Pre-Tape Remarks, December 18, 1989, p. 13.

239. Talmadge, Eric, "Vending Capital of World Finds Good, Bad in Machines," an Associated Press story in *The News-Leader* (Springfield, Missouri), April 28, 1991, p. E1.

240. U.S. Congress Office of Technology Assessment, "International Competition in Services" (OTA-ITE-328). Washington, D.C.: The Author, July 1987.

241. "National Quality Council a Means to Improve U.S. Competitiveness," *Industrial Engineering,* April 1992, p. 7.

242. Elson, John, "Campus of the Future," *Time,* April 13, 1992, p. 55.

243. Morrow, Lane, "Japan in the Mind of America," *Time,* February 10, 1992, p. 18.

244. Castro, Janice, "Work Ethic—In Spades," *Time,* February 17, 1992, p 57.

245. "No Kidding, We're No. 1," *Time,* March 30, 1992, p. 51.

246. Woodbury, Richard, "The Great Energy Bust," *Time,* March 16, 1992, p. 51.

247. "Survey: Japan Work Ethic Making Employee Tired," an Associated Press story in *The News-Leader* (Springfield, Missouri), February 4, 1992, p. 5A.

248. Carnevale, Anthony and Leila J. Gainer, *"The Learning Enterprise,"* Grant No. 99-6-0705-75-079-02. Washington, D.C.: U.S. Department of Labor and American Society for Training and Development, February 1989.

249. Lillard, L. A. and H. W. Tan, "Private Sector Training: Who Gets It and What Are Its Affects?" *Report to the U.S. Department of Labor.* Santa Monica, CA: Rand, 1989.

250. Denison, E. F., "Trends in American Economic Growth," 1929–1982. Washington, DC: The Brookings Institution, 1985.

251. Ricci, Joseph, "Educational Developments and New Opportunities for the 90s," *APICS—The Performance Advantage,* January 1992, p. 12.

252. Albin, John T., "Competing in a Global Market," *APICS—The Performance Advantage,* January 1992, p. 12.

253. Rugman, Alan M. and Alain Verbeke, "Europe 1992 and Competitive Strategies for North American Firms," *Business Horizons* (November–December 1991), p. 73.

254. "More Foreigners at U.S. Colleges," *Fortune,* November 18, 1991, p. 16.

255. "Literacy Skills Training in the Marketplace," *Industrial Engineering,* November 1991, p. 8.

256. Byrne, John A., "Back to School," special report published by *Business Week,* October 28, 1991, p. 106.

257. Denman, Gary L., "Defense Advanced Research Projects Agency," paper presented before the U.S. House of Representatives *Subcommittee on Defense Appropriations Committee,* March 19, 1992, p. 5.

258. Perry, Nancy J., "Where We Go from Here," *Fortune,* October 21, 1991.

259. Henkoff, Ronald, "For States: Reform Turns Radical," *Fortune,* October 21, 1991, p. 137.

260. Alter, Jonathan and Lydia Denworth, "A (Vague) Sense of History," special issue published by *Newsweek,* Fall–Winter 1991, p. 31.

261. Smale, John G., "Challenges and Opportunities in a Shrinking World," talk delivered to *Association of State College and Universities,* Northern Kentucky University, Highland Heights, Kentucky, October 19, 1988, pp. 1–4.

262. Byrne, John A., "The Flap over Executive Pay," *Business Week,* May 6, 1991, p. 93.

263. Perry, Nancy J., "Schools: Tackling the Tough Issues," *Fortune,* December 17, 1990, pp. 143–148.

264. Nussbaum, Bruce, "Needed: Human Capital," *Business Week,* September 19, 1988, pp. 101–103.

265. Bernstein, Aaron, "Where the Jobs Are Is Where the Skills Aren't," *Business Week,* September 19, 1988, p. 108.

266. Ehrlich, Elizabeth and Susan B. Garland, "For American Business, A New World of Workers," special report published by *Business Week,* September 19, 1988, pp. 112–114.

267. Garland, Susan B., "Why the Underclass Can't Get Out from Under," special report published by *Business Week,* September 19, 1988.

268. Ehrlich, Elizabeth, "America's Schools Still Aren't Making the Grade," special report published by *Business Week,* September 19, 1988, p. 132.

269. Richman, Louis, "How America Can Triumph," *Fortune,* December 18, 1989, p. 64.

270. Brownstein, Vivian, "Exporters Will Keep Slugging," *Fortune,* April 20, 1992, p. 23.

271. Solo, Sally, "Japan's U.S. Plants Up 9% in 1991," *Fortune,* April 20, 1992.

272. Waldrop, Judith, "Strong FAX Sales Will Challenge Postal Service," *American Demographics,* Vol. 13, No. 6 (June 1991), p. 12.

273. Edmondson, Brad, "1990 Census Confirms Slower Growth," *American Demographics,* Vol. 13, No. 2 (February 1991), p. 12.

274. Schwartz, Joe and Brad Edmondson, "Privacy Fears Affect Consumer Behavior," *American Demographics,* Vol. 13, No. 2 (February 1991), p. 11.

275. Waldrop, Judith and Thomas Exter, "The Legacy of the 1980s," *American Demographics,* Vol. 13, No. 3 (March 1991), pp. 37–38.

276. Schwartz, Joe, "Americans Annoyed by Wasteful Packaging," *American Demographics,* Vol. 14, No. 4 (April 1992), p. 13.

277. Frankel, Carl, "Blueprint for Green Marketing," *American Demographics,* Vol. 14, No. 4 (April 1992), p. 36.

278. Krafft, Susan, "How to Find Profits in a Recession," *American Demographics,* Vol. 13, No. 1 (January 1991), p. 9.

279. Schwartz, Joe, "Who Knows American Demographics," *American Demographics,* Vol. 13, No. 1 (January 1991), p. 14.

280. Baker, Susannah, "College Cuisine Makes Mother Cringe," *American Demographics,* Vol. 13, No. 9 (September 1991), p. 10.

281. "A Measure of Success," *American Demographics,* Vol. 13, No. 4 (April 1991), p. 9.

282. Schwartz, Joe, "Why Japan's Birthrate Is So Low," *American Demographics,* Vol. 13, No. 4 (April 1991), p. 20.

283. Waldrop, Judith and Joe Schwartz, "New Mexico and Kentucky Beat the Odds," *American Demographics,* Vol. 14, No. 2 (February 1992), p. 9.

284. Helin, David W., "Healthy Families Make Smarter Children," *American Demographics,* Vol. 14, No. 2 (February 1992), p. 13.

285. Wessel, David and Gerald F. Seib, "In Straight-Talking TV Spots, Perot Stretches the Truth to Make His Point," *The Wall Street Journal,* October 28, 1992, p. A18.

286. Riche, Martha Farnsworth, "We're All Minorities Now," *American Demographics,* Vol. 13, No. 10 (October 1991), p. 29.

287. Green, Gordon and Edward Welniak, "The Nine Household Markets," *American Demographics,* Vol. 13, No. 10 (October 1991), p. 38.

288. Demo, Dr., "Billions of Boomers," *American Demographics,* Vol. 14, No. 3 (March 1992), p. 6.

289. Larson, Jan, "A Yen for the U.S.A.," *American Demographics,* Vol. 14, No. 3 (March 1992), p. 46.

290. Cutler, Blayne, "Legions of Lawyers," *American Demographics,* Vol. 13, No. 5 (May 1991), p. 18.

291. Krafft, Susan, "The Demographics of Extra Money," *American Demographics,* Vol. 13, No. 5 (May 1991), p. 20.

292. Crispill, Diane, "Pet Sounds," *American Demographics,* Vol. 13, No. 5 (May 1991), p. 40.

293. Huey, John, "Nothing Is Impossible," *Fortune,* September 23, 1991, p. 140.

294. "50 Million Workers Needed to Handle Needs of Economy," *Industrial Engineering,* Vol. 23, No. 1 (January 1991), p. 8.

295. "Science Education for the Public," *Industrial Engineering,* Vol. 21, No. 10 (October 1989), p. 82.

296. "U.S. Manufacturing Workers 'Underused' by Ineffective Managers," *Industrial Engineering,* Vol. 21, No. 11 (November 1989), p. 6.

297. Martel, Richard, "Reduction in Lead Time Does Make the Difference in Profitable Operations," *Industrial Engineering,* Vol. 21, No. 10 (October 1989), p. 25.

298. "A Future That Didn't Happen," *Industrial Engineering,* Vol. 22, No. 1 (January 1990), p. 80.

299. Seal, Gregory, "1990s—Years of Promise, Years of Peril for U.S. Manufacturers," *Industrial Engineering,* Vol. 22, No. 1 (January 1990), pp. 18–20.

300. "Better Careers for Women," *Industrial Engineering,* Vol. 23, No. 4 (April 1991), p. 80.

301. "Labor Shortages Forecast," *Industrial Engineering,* Vol. 23, No. 5 (May 1991), p. 80.

302. "Unified Europe Largest ACD Market in the 1990s," *Industrial Engineering,* Vol. 23, No. 8 (August 1991), p. 8.

303. "U.S. Salaries Declining," *Industrial Engineering,* Vol. 22, No. 12 (December 1990), p. 80.

304. "To Remain Competitive U.S. Must Exchange Technology, Study Finds," *Industrial Engineering,* Vol. 20, No. 1 (January 1988), p. 4.

305. "Creating Problem-Solvers," *Industrial Engineering,* Vol. 23, No. 8 (August 1991), p. 64.

306. "Companies Fail to Maximize Human Resource Potential," *Industrial Engineering,* Vol. 22, No. 11 (November 1990), pp. 10–12.

307. "High-Tech Industries to Grow Faster than Others, Report Says," *Industrial Engineering,* Vol. 23, No. 4 (April 1991), pp. 8–9.

308. "Federal Beat," *Industrial Engineering,* Vol. 19, No. 7 (July 1987), p. 9.

309. U.S. Department of Commerce, *"Export Programs and Services,"* pamphlet. Washington, D.C.: The Author, p. 2.

310. Tung, Rosalie, "Expatriate Assignments: Enhancing Success and Minimizing Failure," *The Academy of Management Executive,* Vol. 1, No. 2 (May 1987), pp. 117–118.

311. Schweiger, David M., John M. Ivancevich, and Frank R. Power, "Executive Actions for Managing Human Resources Before and After Acquisition," *The Academy of Management Executive,* Vol. 1, No. 2 (May 1987), p. 131.

312. Raelin, Joseph A., "The Professional as the Executive Ethical Aide-de-Camp," *The Academy of Management Executive,* Vol. 1, No. 3 (August 1987), p. 174.

313. Smith, Martin R., "Improving Product Quality in American Industry," *The Academy of Management Executive,* Vol. 1, No. 3 (August 1987), p. 243.

314. Chung, Kae H. and Ronald C. Rogers, "Do Insiders Make Better CEOs than Outsiders," *The Academy of Management Executive,* Vol. 1, No. 4 (November 1987), p. 325.

315. Jacobson, Robert, "The `Austrian' School of Strategy," *Academy of Management Review,* Vol. 17, No. 4 (October 1992), pp. 782–807.

316. Levinson, Harry, "You Won't Recognize Me: Predictions About Changes in Top-Management Characteristics," *The Academy of Management Executive,* Vol. 11, No. 2 (May 1988), p. 119.

317. Luthans, Fred, "Successful Vs. Effective Real Managers," *The Academy of Management Executive,* Vol. 11, No. 2 (May 1988), pp. 130–131.

318. Ulrich, David and Margarethe F. Wirsema, "Gaining Strategic and Organizational Capability in a Turbulent Business Environment," *The Academy of Management,* Vol. 111, No. 2 (May 1989), p. 116.

319. "Business Executives Differ on Business Practice Standards," *APICS—The Performance Advantage* (April 1992), p. 13.

320. Chan, Peng S. and Robert T. Justis, "Franchise Management in East Asia," *The Academy of Management Executive,* Vol. 4, No. 2 (1990), p. 79.

321. "The Checkoff," *The Wall Street Journal,* March 3, 1987, p. 1.

322. Graves, Samuel B. and Sandra A. Waddock, "Institutional Ownership and Control: Implications for Long-Term Corporate

Strategy," *The Academy of Management Executive,* Vol. 4, No. 1 (February 1990), p. 76.

323. Forken, Laura B., "Quality: American, Japanese and Soviet Perspectives," *The Academy of Management Executive,* Vol. 5, No. 4 (November 1991), p. 63.

324. Ives, Blake and Richard O. Mason, "Can Information Technology Revitalize Your Customer Service," *The Academy of Management Executive,* Vol. 4, No. 4 (November 1990), pp. 57–63.

325. Jelinek, Mariann and Nancy J. Adler, "Women: World-Class Managers for Global Competition," *The Academy of Management Executive,* Vol. 1, No. 1 (February 1988).

326. White, B. Joseph, "The Internationalization of Business: One Company's Response," *The Academy of Management Executive,* Vol. 1, No. 1 (February 1988), p. 29.

327. Hill, Charles W. L., Michael A. Hitt, and Robert E. Hoskisson, "Declining U.S. Competitiveness: Reflections on a Crises." *The Academy of Management Executive,* Vol. 1, No. 1 (February 1988), p. 53.

328. Klemkosky, Robert C. "The 1980s: An Evolutionary Decade for the Financial System," *Business Horizons,* Vol. 32, No. 6 (November–December 1989), p. 4.

329. Kensinger, John W. and John D. Martin, "The Decline of Public Equity: The Return to Private Enterprise," *Business Horizons,* Vol. 32, No. 6 (November–December 1989), p. 14.

330. McKenzie, Richard E., "Government Policies in the 1990s," *Business Horizons,* Vol. 33, No. 1 (January–February 1990), p. 27.

331. Ernst, Maurice, "U.S. Exports in the 1990s," *Business Horizons,* Vol. 33, No. 1 (January–February 1990), p. 44.

332. Steingraber, Fred G., "Managing in the 1990s," *Business Horizons,* Vol. 33, No. 1 (January–February 1990), pp. 50–58.

333. Dychtwald, Ken and Greg Gable, "Portrait of a Changing Consumer," *Business Horizons,* Vol. 33, No. 1 (January–February 1990), p. 63.

334. Redwood, Anthony, "Human Resources Management in the 1990s," *Business Horizons,* Vol. 33, No. 1 (January–February 1990), p. 74.

335. Rehder, Robert R., "Japanese Transplants: After the Honeymoon," *Business Horizons,* Vol. 33, No. 1 (January–February 1990), pp. 87–94.

336. Helton, B. Ray, "Coming Home: America at Its Best and Worst," *Industrial Management,* Vol. 31, No. 6 (November–December 1989), pp. 1–7.

337. Resnick, Bruce G., "The Globalization of World Financial Markets," *Business Horizons,* Vol. 32, No. 6 (November–December 1989), p. 34.

338. Miller, Jon D., "The Public Understanding of Science & Technology in the United States, 1990," a report to the National Science Foundation, February 1, 1991, pp. 7–63.

339. Krikland, Richard I., Jr., "What If Japan Triumphs?" *Fortune,* May 18, 1992, pp. 60–62.

340. Curran, John J., "Why Japan Will Emerge Stronger," *Fortune,* May 18, 1992, p. 48.

341. Basadur, Min, "Managing Creativity: A Japanese Model," *The Academy of Management Executive,* Vol. 6, No. 2 (May 1992), p. 32.

342. Kahalas, Harvey and Kathleen Suchon, "Interview with Harold A. Poling Chairman, CEO, Ford Motor Company," *The Academy of Management Executive,* Vol. 6, No. 2 (May 1992), p. 70.

343. Larimer, Tim, "Dysfunction Junction," *USA Weekend,* May 8–10, 1992, p. 5.

344. Woods, Willard, "It's American If Profits Remain Home, Taxes Paid," *The News-Leader* (Springfield, Missouri), May 11, 1992, p. 1D.

345. Whitmire, Richard, "Teen Moms Don't Top Unwed List," *The News-Leader* (Springfield, Missouri), April 17, 1992, p. 7A.

346. Frecka, Thomas J., "AME Accounting Research Project: Accountants Take the Offensive `Just-in-Time,'" *Target AME's Periodical News Service,* Vol. 3, No. 1 (Spring 1987), p. 19.

347. Sutton, Sharon G., "A New Age of Accounting," *Production and Inventory Management Journal,* Vol. 32, No. 1 (First Quarter 1991), p. 73.

348. Barnes, James, Emily T. Smith, Vicki Cahan, Nacomi Freundlich, James E. Ellis, and Joseph Weber, "The Greening of Corporate America," *Business Week,* April 23, 1990, pp. 96–103.

349. Jacobs, Deborah L., "Business Takes on a Green Hue," *The New York Times,* September 2, 1990, Section III, p. 25, cited from James Barnes and Janice Kerry, "Creating a Niche for the Environment in the Business School Curriculum," *Business Horizons,* Vol. 35, No. 2 (March–April 1992), p. 4.

350. Thomas, Lee M., "The Business Community and the Environment: An Important Partnership," *Business Horizons,* Vol. 35, No. 2 (March–April 1992), p. 21.

351. Rosenberg, William G., "The New Clean Air Act of 1990: Winds of Environmental Change," *Business Horizons,* Vol. 35, No. 2 (March–April 1992), p. 34.

352. "The Top 25 Countries: Ranked by Buying Power," *Fortune,* Vol. 122, No. 3, July 30, 1990, p. 104.

353. Fierman, Jaclyn, "Why Women Still Don't Hit the Top," *Fortune,* July 30, 1990, pp. 40–54.

354. Sellers, Patricia, "What Customers Really Want," *Fortune,* June 4, 1990, pp. 59–61.

355. Semich, J. W., "The Cost of Quality," *Purchasing,* Vol. 103, No. 8 (November 5, 1987), p. 61.

356. Saraph, Jayant and Richard J. Sebastian, "Human Resources Strategies for Effective Introduction of Advanced Manufacturing Technologies (AMT)," *Production and Inventory Management Journal,* Vol. 33, No. 1 (First Quarter 1992), p. 64.

357. Magnet, Myron, "The Truth About the American Worker," *Fortune,* May 4, 1992, pp. 50–51.

358. "Today's U.S. Worker," *Fortune,* May 4, 1992, p. 61.

359. "American Workers Are Overworked?" *APICS—The Performance Advantage,* Vol. 2, No. 5 (May 1992), pp. 10–13.

360. Linneman, Robert E. and John L. Stanton, Jr., "Mining for Niches," *Business Horizons,* Vol. 35, No. 3 (May–June 1992), pp. 43–44.

361. Peskin, Myron I. and Francis J. MacGrath, "Industrial Safety: Who Is Responsible and Who Benefits?" *Business Horizons,* Vol. 35, No. 3 (May–June 1992), p. 66.

362. U.S. General Accounting Office, *"Workplace Issues Employment Practices in Selected Large Private Companies,"* report to Congress (GAO/GGD91-47), March 1991, pp. 2–12.

363. U.S. General Accounting Office, *"Water Pollution Greater EPA Leadership Needed to Reduce Nonpoint Source Pollution,"* Report to the Chairman and Ranking Minority Member and Others, U.S. House of Representatives (GAO/RCED–91–10), October 1990, p. 2.

364. U.S. General Accounting Office, *"Workers at Risk Increased Numbers in Contingent Employment Lack Insurance, Other Benefits,"* report to the Chairman, U.S. House of Representatives Subcommittee on Employment and Housing Committee on Government Operations (GAO/HRD-91-56), March 1991, pp. 2–22.

365. U.S. General Accounting Office, *"Transition from School to Work Linking Education and Worksite Training,"* report to Congressional Requesters (GAO/HRD-91-105), August 1991, pp. 2–18.

366. U.S. General Accounting Office, *"Employee Stock Ownership Plans Participants Benefits Generally Increased but Many Plans Terminated,"* report to the Chairman, U.S. House of Representatives

Subcommittee on Labor-Management Relations, Committee on Education and Labor (GAO/HRD-91-28), December 1990, p. 3.

367. Wolfe, Art, "The Corporate Apology," *Business Horizons,* Vol. 33, No. 2 (March–April 1990), p. 10.

368. U.S. General Accounting Office, *"Foreign Investment Concerns in the U.S. Real Estate Sector During the 1980s,"* report to the Chairman, U.S. House of Representatives Subcommittee on Oversight and Investigations Committee on Energy and Commerce (GAO/NSIAD-91-140), June 1991, pp. 2-27.

369. Frazier, Franklin, *Child Labor: The Characteristics of Working Children in the United States,* statement before the U.S. Senate Subcommittee on Labor Committee, on Labor and Human Resources and Subcommittee on Children, Family and Drugs and Alcoholism Committee on Labor and Human Resources (GAO/T-HRD-91-13), March 19, 1991, p. 2.

370. U.S. General Accounting Office, *"International Trade Comparison of U.S. and Foreign Antidumping Practices,"* report to Congressional Requesters (GAO/NSIAD-91-59), November 1990, p. 8.

371. U.S. General Accounting Office, *"Foreign Investment Japanese-Affiliated Automakers' 1989 U.S. Productions Impact on Jobs,"* report to Congressional Requesters (GAO/NSIAD-91-52), October 1990, pp. 1-2.

372. U.S. General Accounting Office, *"Internal Revenue Service Employee Views on Integrity and Willingness to Report Misconduct,"* fact sheet for the Chairman, U.S. House of Representatives Subcommittee on Commerce Consumer and Monetary Affairs, Committee on Government Operations (GAO/GGD-91-112FS), July 1991, p. 2.

373. Brockner, Joel, "Managing the Effects of Layoffs on Survivors," *California Management Review,* Vol. 34, No. 2 (Winter 1992), p. 16.

374. Aaker, David A., "How Will the Japanese Compete in Retail Services?" *California Management Review,* Vol. 33, No. 1 (Fall 1990), pp. 54–58.

375. Pfeffer, Jeffrey, "Understanding Power in Organizations." *California Management Review,* Vol. 34, No. 2 (Winter 1992), p. 33, cited from Jeffrey Gandz and Victor V. Murray, "The Experience of Workplace Politics," *Academy of Management Journal,* Vol. 23 (1980), pp. 237–251.

376. Garrison, Stephen A., "Wanted: Eight Million Educated Workers," *Fortune,* March 26, 1990, p. 56.

250 ■ References

377. Bergsten, C. Fred, "The World Economy After the Cold War," *California Management Review,* Vol. 34, No. 2 (Winter 1992), pp. 52–62.

378. Yao-Sutty, "Global or Stateless Corporations Are National Firms with International Operations," *California Management Review,* Vol. 34, No. 2 (Winter 1992), pp. 109–119.

379. Turner, John N., "There Is More to Trade than Trade: An Analysis of the U.S./Canada Trade Agreement 1988," *California Management Review,* Vol. 33, No. 2 (Winter 1991), p. 108.

380. Gunish, Dawn, "Women a Rarity in Executive Training," *Personnel Journal,* Vol. 71, No. 5 (May 1992), p. 16.

381. Gunish, Dawn, "The ADA's Effect on Existing Employees," *Personnel Journal,* Vol. 71, No. 4 (April 1992), p. 16.

382. O'Toole, James, "Do Good, Do Well: The Business Enterprise Trust Awards," *California Management Review,* Vol. 33, No. 3 (Spring 1991), p. 23.

383. "An American Vision for the 1990s," *Fortune,* March 26, 1990, p. 14.

384. Perot, Ross, "How to Make the U.S. Bulletproof," *Fortune,* March 26, 1990, p. 32.

385. Petre, Peter, "Lifting American Competitiveness," *Fortune,* April 23, 1990, p. 56.

386. Gustke, Constance A., "Making Big Gains from Small Steps," *Fortune,* April 23, 1990, p. 119.

387. Jacob, Rahul, "Oil Imports: U.S. `Deeper in the Hole,'" *Fortune,* February 12, 1990, p. 9.

388. "Japan's Unhappy Auto Workers," *Fortune,* October 22, 1990, p. 10.

389. Thor, Carl, "Thor's Thoughts," Letter (American Productivity & Quality Center), Vol. 10, No. 1 (July 1990), p. 4.

390. "CEOs Assess U.S. Economy," *Letter* (American Productivity & Quality Center), Vol. 10, No. 1 (July 1990), p. 4.

391. Thor, Carl., "Thor's Thoughts," *Letter* (American Productivity & Quality Center), Vol. 10, No. 2 (August 1990), p. 2.

392. "Dealing with Change: Motorola University Has the Learning Spirit," *Letter* (American Productivity & Quality Center), Vol. 10, No. 8 (February 1991), pp. 1–6.

393. Summers, Timothy P. and Jeffrey S. Harrison, "Alliances for Success," *Training & Development,* Vol. 46, No. 3 (March 1992), p. 70.

394. Hayes, F. Dale, "Training the Next Generation," *Training & Development,* Vol. 45, No. 12 (December 1991), p. 14.

395. Rossett, Allison and Kevin Krumdieck, "How Trainers Score on Quality," *Training & Development,* Vol. 46, No. 1 (January 1992), p. 14.

396. Thomsen, Stephen, "We Are All `US,'" *Columbia Journal of World Business,* Vol. 26, No. 4 (Winter 1992), pp. 6–19.

397. U.S. General Accounting Office, "Sweatshops in the U.S." briefing report to Honorable Charles E. Schumer, U.S. House of Representatives (GAO/HRD-88-130BR), August 1988, pp. 8–9.

398. "Ain't No Mountain High Enough," *Fortune,* June 1, 1992, p. 14.

399. "Slower Payoff for B-School Grads," *Fortune,* June 1, 1992 p. 17.

400. Erdmann, Peter, "Editor's Note," *Columbia Journal of World Business,* Vol. 26, No. 4 (Winter 1992), p. 4.

401. Yoshida, Kosaku, "New Economic Principles in America— Competition and Cooperation." *Columbia Journal of World Business,* Vol. 26, No. 4 (Winter 1992), p. 34.

402. Beim, David O., "Why Are Banks Dying," *Columbia Journal of World Business,* Vol. 27, No. 1 (Spring 1992), p. 7.

403. Whitehouse, Herbert A., "How Pension Investment Policy Drains American Economic Strength," *Columbia Journal of World Business,* Vol. 27, No. 1 (Spring 1992), p. 23.

404. Vandermerve, Sandra and Michael D. Oliff, "Corporate Challenges for an Age of Reconsumption," *Columbia Journal of World Business,* Vol. 26, No. 3 (Fall 1991), p. 8.

405. *International Management* (August 1990), cited in Sandra Vandermerve and Michael D. Oliff, "Corporate Challenges for an Age of Reconsumption," Columbia Journal of World Business, Vol. 26, No. 3 (Fall 1991), p. 8.

406. *World Link,* No. 2 (1991), cited in Sandra Vandermerve and Michael D. Oliff, "Corporate Challenges for an Age of Reconsumption," *Columbia Journal of World Business,* Vol. 26, No. 3 (Fall 1991), p. 8.

407. The prognosis is given by Jean Marie Pelt, *L'Homme Retaure* (Paris: Editions du Sevil, 1990), cited in Sandra Vandermerve and Michael D. Oliff, "Corporate Challenges for an Age of Reconsumption," *Columbia Journal of World Business,* Vol. 26, No. 3 (Fall 1991), p. 10.

408. Negroponte, John D., "Continuity and Change in U.S. Mexican Relations," *Columbia Journal of World Business,* Vol. 26, No. 2 (Summer 1991), p. 9.

409. Wu, Terry and Neil Longley, "The U.S.–Canada Free Trade Agreement," *Columbia Journal of World Business,* Vol. 26, No. 2 (Summer 1991), p. 61.

410. French, Hilary F. "Green Revolutions: Environmental Reconstruction in Eastern Europe and the Soviet Union," *Columbia Journal of World Business,* Vol. 26, No. 1 (Spring 1991), pp. 28–33.

411. Schachter, Jim, "US Technology—As a Giant Does, Ideas Tiptoe Away," *Los Angeles Times,* Part I (February 21, 1988), cited in Kosaku Yoshida, "Deming Management Philosophy: Does It Work in the U.S. as Well as in Japan?" *Columbia Journal of World Business,* Vol. 24, No. 3 (Fall 1989), p. 14.

412. Doyle, Frank P., "People Power: The Global Human Resource Challenge for the 90s," *Columbia Journal of World Business,* Vol. 25, Nos. 1 and 2 (Spring–Summer 1990), p. 37.

413. Engineering Manpower Commission of American Association of Engineering Societies, Inc., "Engineering & Technology Enrollments: Fall 1988," report published in 1989 and cited in Frank P. Doyle, "People Power: The Global Human Resource Challenge for the 90s," *Columbia Journal of World Business,* Vol. 25, Nos. 1 and 2 (Spring–Summer 1990), p. 37.

414. National Science Foundation, *Science and Engineering Research Benefits* (NSF91-57). Washington, D.C.: The Author.

415. McCartney, James, "Buy American Only a Sellout to Politics," *Washington State Journal,* February 2, 1992, p. 1C.

416. Peterson, Esther, "Your Life Is on the Line—Sobering Facts," *Consumer Watch Bulletin* (National Association of Professional Insurance Agents).

417. Smith, Brian W., *The Insurance Industry: A Key Player in the U.S. Economy,* 3rd ed.:Alliance of American Insurers, Schaumburg, Illinois,1990.

418. Mendelowitz, Allan I., of the U.S. General Accounting Office, "Comprehensive Quality Management," statement to the U.S. House of Representatives Subcommittee in Science, Research and Technology Committee on Science, Space and Technology (GAO/T–NSIAD–90–22), March 20, 1990.

419. U.S. General Accounting Office, *"Global Warming: Emission Reductions Possible as Scientific Uncertainties Are Resolved,"* report to the Chairman, U.S. House of Representatives Environment, Energy and Natural Resources Subcommittee, Committee on Government Operations (GAO/RCED-90-58), September 1990.

420. U.S. General Accounting Office, *"Health Insurance a Profile of the Uninsured in Michigan and the United States,"* report to the Chairman, U.S. Senate Subcommittee on Health for Families and the Uninsured Committee on Finance (GAO/HRD-90-97), May 1990.

421. U.S. General Accounting Office, "*Health Insurance: Availability and Adequacy for Small Business,*" statement before the U.S. House of Representatives Subcommittee on Health and the Environment Committee on Energy and Commerce (GAO/T-HRD-90-02), October 16, 1989.

422. U.S. General Accounting Office, "*Quality Assurance: A Comprehensive National Strategy for Health Care Is Needed,*" briefing report to the Chairman, U.S. Bipartisan Commission on Comprehensive Health Care (GAO/PEMD-90-14BR), February 1990.

423. U.S. General Accounting Office, "*Health Insurance: Cost Increases Lead to Coverage Limitations and Cost Shifting,*" report to Congressional Requesters (GAO/HRD-90-68), May 1990.

424. U.S. General Accounting Office, "*Dislocated Workers: Labor-Management Committees Enhance Reemployment Assistance,*" (GAO/HRD-90-3), November 1989.

425. U.S. General Accounting Office, "*U.S. and Foreign Strategies for Preparing Noncollege Youth for Employment,*" Statement by Franklin Frazier, Director of Education and Employment Issues Human Resources Division before the Subcommittee on Education and Health Joint Economic Committee (GAO/T-HRD-90-31), June 14, 1990.

426. U.S. General Accounting Office, "*Occupational Safety And Health: Options for Improving Safety and Health in the Workplace,*" briefing report to the U.S. House of Representatives Subcommittee on Health and Safety, Committee on Education and Labor (GAO/HRD-90-66BR), August 1990.

427. McCartney, James, "Buy American Only a Sellout to Politics," *Wisconsin State Journal,* Sunday, February 2, 1992, p. 1C.

428. Fatsis, Stefan and Bart Ziegler, "Made in U.S.A. Goods Include International Stops," an Associated Press story in *Wisconsin State Journal,* February 2, 1992, p. 2C.

429. Joderstrom, Susan and Leonard B. Kruk, *Administrative Support Systems and Procedures. Cincinnati,* OH: South-Western, 1992.

430. Javna, John, "Health Care Security, Jobs All Pressing Environmental Issues," *The News-Leader* (Springfield, Missouri), July 11, 1992, p. C1.

431. Dobson, Allen and Richard L. Clarke, "Shifting No Solution to Problem of Increasing Costs," *Health Care Financial Management,* July 1992, p. 25.

432. U.S. General Accounting Office, "Product Liability: Verdicts and Case Resolution in Five States," report to the Chairman, U.S. House of Representatives Subcommittee on Commerce, Consumer

Protection, and Competitiveness Committee on Energy & Commerce (GAO/HRD-89-99), September 1989, p. 10.

433. U.S. General Accounting Office, "Foreign Investment: Trends in Foreign Ownership of U.S. Farmland and Commercial Real Estate," fact sheet for the Honorable Quentin N. Burdick, U.S. Senate (GAO/NS1AD-89-168FS), July 1989, pp. 2–4.

434. "Service-Producing Industries Should Lead in Growth of Science/Engineering Jobs Through the Year 2000," *Science Resources Studies Highlights,* National Science Foundation, December 30, 1988, p. 13.

435. U.S. General Accounting Office, "Vocational Education: Opportunities to Prepare for the Future," report to Chairman, U.S. House of Representative Subcommittee on Elementary, Secondary, and Vocational Education, Committee on Education and Labor (GAO/HRD-89-55), May 1989, p. 10.

436. National Science Foundation, "Science and Technology Report and Outlook 1985–1988," Office of Science and Technology Policy, January 13, 1989, p. 3.

437. "Canadians, Not Edison, Invented Light Bulb," *Eureka,* Spring 1992, pp. 4–5.

438. Bartholome, Lloyd W., "Preparing Business Education for the 21st Century," *Business Education Forum,* December 1991, p. 16.

439. Florida, Richard and David Browdy, "How Westinghouse Let Another One Get Away," *Business & Society Review,* No. 80, Winter 1992, pp. 19–27.

440. Zack, Jeffrey, "Ethics in the News," *Business and Society Review,* No. 80, Winter 1992, pp. 5–6.

441. Zack, Jeffrey, "Ethics in the News, *Business and Society Review,* No. 87, Summer 1992, pp. 4–5.

442. Pavee, Irene, "Older Workers Face Age-Old Problem," *Business and Society Review,* No. 77, Spring 1991, p. 26.

443. Moore, Stephen, "Immigration Policy: Open Minds on Open Borders," *Business and Society Review,* No. 77, Spring 1991, p. 39.

444. Kanter, Donald L. and Philip H. Mirvis, "Cynicism: The New American Malaise," *Business and Society Review,* No. 77, Spring 1991, p. 58.

445. Brenner, Brian and Joseph Weber, "A Spicier Stew in the Melting Pot," *Business Week,* December 21, 1992, pp. 29–30.

446. Knight, Jerry, statement made on National Public Radio, October 10, 1992.

447. Ibbotson Associates, Inc., *Stocks, Bonds, Bills, and Inflation 1991 Yearbook.* : The Author, 1991, based on Exhibit 39 in the titled work, the 1991 yearbook, Chicago, Illinois.

448. Datastream, Ibbotson Associates, and Sanford C. Bernstein and Company, undated.

449. Barro, Robert J., "Keynes Is Still Dead," *The Wall Street Journal,* October 29, 1992, p. A14.

450. Stuller, Jay, "The Rush of the Times," *Kiwanis,* June–July 1992, pp. 22–25.

451. Tully, Shawn, "America's Painful Doctor Shortage," *Fortune,* November 16, 1992, pp. 103–112.

452. "Harper's Index," *Harper's Magazine,* Vol. 285, No. 1710 (November 1992), p. 15.

453. Port, Otis, John Carey, Kevin Kelly, and Stephanie A. Forest, "Quality: Small and Midsize Companies Seize the Challenge—Not a Moment Too Soon," *Business Week,* November 30, 1992, pp. 66–72.

454. Fefer, Mark D., "Time to Speed up the S&L Cleanup," *Fortune,* November 16, 1992, pp. 116–120.

455. Jacob, Rahul, "India Is Opening for Business," *Fortune,* November 16, 1992, pp. 128–130.

456. Ramsey, Nancy, "How Business Can Help the Schools," *Fortune,* November 16, 1992, pp. 147–174.

457. Koretz, Gene, "The Fed May Be Facing a No-Win Situation," *Business Week,* October 26, 1992, p. 22.

458. Labich, Kenneth, "Europe's Sky Wars," *Fortune,* November 2, 1992, pp. 88–91.

459. Kirkpatrick, David, "Hot New PC Services," *Fortune,* November 2, 1992, pp. 108–114.

460. Spiers, Joseph, "Let's Get Real About Taxes," *Fortune,* October 19, 1992, pp. 78–81.

461. Norton, Rob, "Taking on Public Enemy No. 1," *Fortune,* October 19, 1992, pp. 84–87.

462. Smith, Lee, "The Right Cure for Health Care," *Fortune,* October 19, 1992, pp. 88–89.

463. Thornton, Emily, "Japanese Bank Goes to the Dogs," *Fortune,* October 19, 1992, pp. 17–18.